THE ALPHA
AND
THE OMEGA

THE ALPHA AND
THE OMEGA

A RESTATEMENT OF
THE CHRISTIAN HOPE
IN CHRIST'S COMING

PAUL ERB

HERALD PRESS
SCOTTDALE, PENNSYLVANIA

LIBRARY OF CONGRESS CATALOGUE CARD NUMBER 55-10561
PRINTED IN THE UNITED STATES OF AMERICA

THE CONTENTS OF THIS VOLUME CONSTITUTED
THE CONRAD GREBEL LECTURES FOR 1955

THE CONRAD GREBEL
LECTURES

The Conrad Grebel Lectureship was set up for the purpose of making possible an annual study by a Mennonite scholar of some topic of interest and value to the Mennonite Church and to other Christian people. It is administered by a committee appointed by and responsible to the General Educational Council of the Mennonite Board of Education. This committee appoints the lecturers, approves their subjects, counsels them during their study, and arranges for the delivery of the lectures at one or more places.

The Lectureship is financed by donors who contribute annually $500 each.

Conrad Grebel was an influential leader in the sixteenth-century Swiss Anabaptist movement and is thought of as one of the founders of the Mennonite Church. Because of the direction which he gave to the movement, this Lectureship has been named for him.

Lectures thus far delivered are as follows:

PREFACE

The present volume consists of the 1955 Conrad Grebel Lectures, delivered at Hesston College, Goshen College, and Orrville, Ohio. The author acknowledges helpful criticisms and reactions from the Conrad Grebel Lectureship Committee and from many who heard the lectures or read them in manuscript. He is greatly indebted, too, to the many books and articles which have recently appeared on related themes.

These lectures are intended to make some helpful contribution to the increased current discussion of eschatology. It is hoped particularly that they will lift the discussion of unfulfilled prophecy out of the profitless argument between different schools of thought into which it has so often fallen. If we can forget our classifications and our embattled terminology, we may achieve unity in a fresh approach and a new terminology that is nearer to the Scriptures, our only source of knowledge concerning God's plan for the future.

It is unfortunate that the controversies concerning the interpretation of eschatology have driven many people away from the subject. Some ministers, despairing of finding a common ground upon which all believers can stand, have not been preaching on eschatology. And so an important area of doctrine has fallen into neglect, and many church attendants are ignorant of vital truth which they should know.

It is the author's hope that this volume will discourage the preaching of speculative, controversial prophetic themes, and encourage the preaching of the certain eschatology on which the Bible speaks with clarity and authority.

The theological concepts here presented may offer difficulties to lay readers. The author suggests, if the reader finds difficulties in understanding Part I, that he go to Part II, which is the heart of the lectures. Here the main thesis, stated in Part I, finds its supporting argument. Part I may be more easily read after Parts II and III.

Vocabulary is a problem here. The subject has been so neglected that the very words which the subject requires are not understood by many readers. Therefore, with apologies for defining what may be well known to many, we offer the following glossary.

1. *Alpha and Omega.* The first and last letters of the Greek alphabet. The A and the Z, the beginning and the ending.

2. *Apocalyptic.* A manner of speaking or writing which makes large use of images and symbols.

3. *Chiliasm.* The doctrine of a thousand-year reign of Christ upon the earth; millennialism.

4. *Denouement* (de-noo'mä). A French term used to describe the unfolding at the end of a plot, when everything becomes clear and the action reaches its end.

5. *Eschatology.* The study of "last things," of events of the end-time.

6. *Eschaton.* Greek for "the last," "the end."

7. *Parousia* (paroo'sia). The Anglicized Greek word often used in the New Testament for the Second Advent of Christ.

8. *Telos.* Greek for "the end," "the goal."

9. *Tension.* Strain which results when one needs at the same time to look two ways, both back to the work of Christ at His first coming and the present effects of that work, and forward to what He will do when He comes again.

All Bible quotations, unless otherwise specified, are from the American Standard Version (Thomas Nelson and Sons, 1901).

May 2, 1955   PAUL ERB

CONTENTS

PART I

THE STUDY OF ESCHATOLOGY

I

THE BEGINNING
THE MIDDLE
AND THE END

"I am the Alpha and the Omega, the first and the last, the beginning and the end."[1] These were the words of the Lord to John, the Revelator. Our Lord Jesus Christ was in the beginning with God, participating in the creation. In the fullness of time He was made flesh and dwelt among us on earth, revealing the Father and accomplishing our redemption. And at the end of time He will come again to complete all that is involved in that redemption. He is the beginning, the end, and everything in between. He is indeed the A and the Z, the Alpha and the Omega.

A dramatic plot, said the Greek philosopher Aristotle, should picture an action complete and whole. "A whole is that which has beginning, middle, and end," he continued. And although that seems obvious, he went on to define these three essential parts of a plot. "A beginning is that which does not itself follow anything by causal necessity, but after which something naturally is or comes to be." That is, it is a beginning which starts something. "An end," went on Aristotle, "is that which itself naturally follows some other thing, either by necessity or in the regular course of events, but has nothing following it." That is, it ends something

1 Rev. 22:13.

1

which has been begun. Aristotle concludes, "A middle is that which follows something as some other thing follows it."[2] The middle is essential action which leads naturally from a beginning to an ending. Early in that course of action comes what literary critics have called an inciting force, which creates the complication or problem that must be worked out. And somewhere in the middle the action comes to a climax, which determines the end which must be reached. Just at the end comes the denouement, the unfolding of the plot which reveals just how the problem has been solved. The plot has not been completed until this denouement has been reached. It requires more than a beginning and a middle to make a drama. There must also be a logical end.

The history of the world, which centers about God's dealings with man, has often been likened to a drama. The story of man's creation, fall, and redemption has been called "the greatest drama ever staged."[3] Vos says, "It is drama . . . hastening on with accelerated movement to the point of denouement and consummation."[4] And the drama is all the more intense and impressive because it is not an imitation, but is real history; the persons of the drama are not play actors but include the Trinity, the angels, good and bad, and all the people who walk this great stage, the earth, from the beginning to the end of time.

Now this great drama, as we have seen, must have a beginning, a middle, and an end. Its beginning is the creation of the world and of man by the powerful act of God. God's purpose in the creation was His glory. And the glory of God involves also the happiness and glory of His creatures. Early

---

[2] Aristotle, "The Nature of Tragedy," *The Poetics.*
[3] Quoted by W. A. Whitehouse, "The Modern Discussion of Eschatology," in *Eschatology* (Oliver and Boyd, Edinburgh, 1952).
[4] Geerhardus Vos, *Pauline Eschatology* (Eerdmans, 1952), p. 26.

in the action comes the opposition of Satan, the enemy of God, an opposition which continues to the Denouement at the end of time. God purposes the eternal blessedness of man; Satan purposes his downfall and ruin. Man is tempted and falls into sin—a sin whose penalty is death. But God has a counterplan for man's redemption, and makes the first of many promises of a coming Redeemer, who shall save man from sin and death.

When the knowledge of the true God has well-nigh disappeared from the earth, the Book of Genesis tells us how God calls Abraham to become the father of a chosen people, who shall become His means of revelation and redemption. He gives Abraham a son in his old age, and covenants with Abraham to make him a great nation through whom all the families of the earth shall be blessed. When the descendants of Abraham become enslaved in Egypt, God delivers them with a mercy and power which makes the exodus from Egypt a great type of the salvation which shall save God's people in the later days. Having grown from a family to a theocratic nation, Israel is given a system of sacrifices, laws, and ordinances which also point forward to a coming redemption. The nation is taught to look for a Messiah who shall become their Saviour. Another intimation of future developments is seen when David the king of Israel is promised an everlasting kingdom, with a Son of David upon his throne forever.

The prophets come upon the stage one after another to call the people to righteousness and to build up together the picture of events to come. They add their various details to the concept of the Messiah who shall come, and of the kingdom over which He shall rule. The picture of the Messianic Kingdom to come is fragmentary and incomplete. It is a picture in time, not in eternity, with the Kingdom established for God's people upon this earth. The means are not clear, but the hope is certain. It rests upon the divine promise, and will be brought about by the divine act. The restoration of the Davidic dynasty will bring a new age of peace and righteousness. Though the picture on the whole is in an earthly setting, there are not lacking details which point to a spiritual kingdom. The new covenant will be written in hearts, not in the flesh. God's Spirit will be poured out upon all, so that righteousness will proceed from an inner motivation, not from an outer compulsion. And the sublimest heights of Old Testament prophecy are reached in Isaiah's vision of the Suffering Servant who, not as a conquering hero, but by self-denying love and sacrifice, will carry to its climax God's redemptive purpose for the sinful race of men.

The backdrop of the prophetic message is the sordid history of moral failure which made necessary the judgment and the destruction of Samaria and Jerusalem, the exile under the conquering tyrants, the end of the theocracy. But the threat of national extinction does not quench the light of faith. The hope of a future according to the promise of God never dies. There is the heroic return of a remnant to the rubble which was Jerusalem, the rebuilding of the temple, the restoration of its worship, and the renewal of the waiting for the reign of a Messiah. "These three beliefs," says John Bright, "are constants of Israel's faith; that God controls history and in it reveals His righteous judgment and saving power; that God has a purpose in history toward which history tends—the establishment of His kingdom over His people."[5] Just how and when He will do this the Old Testament does not say. But since it "describes itself as an

5 John Bright, "Faith and Destiny," *Interpretation*, January, 1951.

open door leading toward greater deeds of God (which He will do when He fulfills all His words), therefore we are invited by the very letter of the Old Testament to look and go through this open door."[6]

In this very brief summary we have come far into the middle of the eschatological drama. But we are still waiting for any decisive action which can be considered a climax. The action is rising to a height not yet attained. We are still in the era of promise and expectation, with nothing of fulfillment except the tentative judgments along the way. S. D. F. Salmond says, "This eschatology of the Old Testament, which grew from less to more in the course of Israel's history, remained nevertheless incomplete at its highest, and pointed to something beyond itself. The eschatology of the New Testament became its heir, passing beyond its limits and carrying its principles to their issues."[7] The Old Testament message closes because words can go no farther. The plot calls for new deeds, and that requires a new person on the scene. As A. G. Hebert puts it, "The Old Testament is at once the word of God and not the final word of God. It is an imperfect, provisional, preparatory covenant, needing to be made complete in the Messiah. It represents a stage in the education of the People of God. . . . The conceptions of the Old Testament writers are imperfect and incomplete . . . because the word which God was speaking through each of them was . . . fragmentary and partial. The Messianic Idea in its wholeness is complete and true, but it is only when the Messiah comes that it can be seen as a whole."[8]

6 Marcus Barth, "The Christ in Israel's History," *Theology Today*, October, 1954.

7 S. D. F. Salmond, "Eschatology in the New Testament," *Hastings Bible Dictionary*.

8 A. G. Hebert, *The Throne of David* (Faber and Faber, London, 1941), pp. 241 f.

2

And so we come to that moment in the drama of redemption in which God comes on the scene in the person of the God-Man, the Son of David who is the promised Messiah. God's self-revelation in the person of His Son is the turning point, "the axis of all history."[9] This is the mid-point in the time line of the present age. Here, as at the creation, the beginning, God touched our world, and His touch was world-shaking in its effects. Here the eternal entered and transformed the temporal. "The center of Christianity is the faith that the eternal world has broken into time in Jesus as the Christ."[10] Christ came to fulfill the promise of redemption, the Messianic expectation, the prophecy of an eternal Kingdom. Being in His essential nature both the Origin and the End of history, the Alpha and the Omega of God's purpose and plan for man's salvation in time and eternity, He begins that series of utterances and acts which sum up all that God would say to us and do for us.

When He is born of the Virgin, the angelic announcement shows that the Babe is God in the flesh. Come to maturity, He proclaims that the Kingdom has arrived. He claims deity, and proves His claims by His words of truth and His deeds of power. But His people had crystallized their concept of the promised Redeemer as a political leader who would free them from the Romans and set up an earthly throne. They rejected Jesus and hounded Him to an ignominious death on a Roman cross. To the casual observer, as indeed even to those few disciples who had believed on Him, the divine intervention seems to have been only a futile gesture. Sin and Satan seem to be triumphant and the history of mankind to be in a complete chaos. God's

9 Karl Jaspers, *The Origin and Goal of History* (Yale U. Press, 1953).

10 A. Roy Eckardt, "Land of Promise and City of God," *Theology Today*, January, 1954.

attempt has failed. There is no redemption from sin and death, no cure for human ills, no hope for a better day. The Messiah who was to come, the King who was to reign forever, is dead. It is history's darkest moment.

But Easter morning utterly reverses all that. The miraculous and glorious resurrection brings new light and hope. God is proved to be the Lord of history after all. After Easter the cross is seen to be "the supreme moment in the history of the universe—the death of its Creator as an atonement for the sin of man."[11] Christ's disciples came to see that here, and not on some international battlefield, was fought the decisive battle between God and Satan. Here was signed the death warrant of all the forces which were opposing God and trying to drag mankind down to ruin. This victory became clear to the disciples as Jesus explained to them after the Resurrection, and in the Spirit-taught days after Pentecost, the meaning of all the prophecies concerning Him. They learned to think of Easter as that crucial point in time when the battle of the ages was won, when therefore the New Age of their Messiah-Redeemer began. The Resurrection is the sign that the power of God is able to do all that He wants to do, and that the promised deliverance has come. The Resurrection communicates an assurance that evil is no longer irresistible, that Satan's power now has limits. It is now clear "that God, in Christ, has redeemed the world from all powers of sin and evil which had hitherto been a wall separating man from God."[12] There is assurance that the triumphant reign of God has begun. In this faith "man is now free to face a future that belongs to God."[13]

11 Philip Mauro, *A Short Exposition of Seventy Weeks Prophecy* (Perry Studio, Washington, 1933), p. 33.

12 F. G. Denbeaux, "Biblical Hope," *Interpretation,* July, 1951.

13 *Ibid.*

The resurrected Christ soon went away to be seated at the right hand of the Father. His disciples, however, had received His promise that He would be with them to the end of the age. A beginning in the fulfillment of that promise came when the Holy Spirit fell upon His faithful followers as they were praying in the upper room at Jerusalem. This became the norm for believers—living and serving in the power of the Spirit. They were living "in Christ"—with all His resources and grace available for their need. Though they were at home in Jerusalem or Antioch or Ephesus, they actually were living in "the heavenlies" with their risen and ascended Lord. The life of Christ's church, which came into being at Pentecost, was an ecstatic, triumphant experience because its members had been translated out of a worldly kingdom into the Kingdom of God's dear Son. They were already tasting the joys of a world yet to come.

A terrible judgment came upon the Jewish people as retribution for their rejection of the heaven-sent Messiah. Jerusalem was utterly destroyed in A.D. 70 by the Romans. Josephus wrote: "there was left nothing to make those who had come thither believe it had ever been inhabited."[14] Thousands of Jews were cruelly slaughtered, and others were carried away as slaves. "The destruction of Jerusalem signalized that the old dispensation was over and never to return," says J. M. Kik. He continues: ". . . the destruction of Jerusalem and its Temple was a great blessing for the rest of the world. . . . The spiritual conception of the Kingdom taught by Christ and the apostles would have been much more difficult to teach if the old city and old Temple had not been totally destroyed."[15]

14 Quoted by J. M. Kik, *Matthew Twenty-four* (Bible Truth Depot, Swengel, Pa., 1948), p. 28.

15 J. M. Kik, *op. cit.*, pp. 21 f.

The Jewish people were dispersed among all nations so that for centuries there were but few in the ancestral land. The church became God's chosen people, but chosen in Christ from both Jew and Gentile. The Gospel was preached, as Christ has commanded, throughout all the world, so that church was composed of many races and tongues. Satan opposed this expansion in every way he could, sometimes by inciting unbelievers to persecution of the Christians, and sometimes by entering into the life and thought of the church and defeating the testimony by error, by worldliness, and by sin. But though his success was enormous, the light of the truth was never extinguished. The true Kingdom of God's saints always found its succession in the hearts of the faithful. The Kingdom was growing, in that in every generation thousands believed. But the wheat grew among the tares, and false concepts always threatened the true life in the Spirit.

It is very clear to the student of the New Testament and of Christian history that the people of God ever since Easter and Pentecost have lived under tension. It is the tension between the present and the future, the now and the then, the already and the not yet. The Kingdom has come, but is yet to come; the Christian lives in the Spirit, but has experienced only the earnest of that spiritual existence which is yet future; he lives in Christ and enjoys His daily presence, and yet he looks for the return of the Saviour from heaven; he has eternal life now, but expects at the end of the age a different state of immortality; he lives now in the power of the resurrection, but waits to be delivered from mortality; he lives in this present age, but has already tasted of things that belong to an age to come; in the communion memorial he looks back to the work of Christ upon the cross, but also forward to a second coming, knowing that he memorializes the death only "till he come"[16]; he rejoices in a present salvation, yet waits for a salvation yet to be revealed. The church stands in an intermediate position between the middle and the end. There is both fulfillment and accomplishment at that great mid-point and climax of the drama of redemption when Jesus Christ by His death and resurrection introduced into the world a great, new thing which has affected men as nothing else ever has. It was the mighty act of God, revealing His righteousness and love, and making our justification and sanctification possible. But there is also hope and anticipation. The work of God is not yet complete. The last *days* in which we already are require a last *day,* the end of time. God has spoken, but the New Testament makes it clear that He has not spoken His last word.

No truth is more important than this for the study of eschatology. John A. T. Robinson says, ". . . the Christian era and the Christian life are viewed in the New Testament as set between two poles, between the fact that the end has come and the fact that the end is yet to be."[17] Oscar Cullmann puts it thus: ". . . the tension between 'this age' and the 'coming age' . . . results from the fact that . . . the present of the church already lies in the new age, and yet is before the Parousia, and so before the actual end time. . . . It is already the time of the end, and yet is not *the* end. This tension finds expression in the entire theology of Primitive Christianity. The present period of the church is the time between the decisive battle which has already occurred, and the 'Victory Day.' To anyone who does not take account of this tension, the entire New Testament is a book with seven seals, for this tension is the silent presupposition that lies behind all that it says."[18]

16 I Cor. 11:26.
17 J. A. T. Robinson, *In the End God* (Clark, London, 1952), p. 61.
18 Oscar Cullmann, *Christ and Time* (Westminster, 1950), pp. 145 f.

T. A. Kantonen also describes this tension: ". . . the present blessings constantly point to still greater glories in the future. The church is in the paradoxical position of having to fight a battle which has already been won. Inwardly united by the Spirit with its triumphant Lord, it is nevertheless outwardly separated from Him and engaged in agonized combat with the defeated powers of the present evil age. In this situation it is not strange that the hope of the church should take the form of an intense longing for the speedy consummation of its Lord's triumph, the Parousia."[19]

John Howard Yoder shows how the church faces two ways at the same time: "The New Testament sees our present age, the age of the church, extending from Pentecost to the Parousia, as a period of the overlapping of two aeons. These aeons are not distinct periods of time, for they exist at the same moment. They differ rather in nature or direction; one points backward to human history outside of (before) Christ; the other points forward to the fullness of the Kingdom of God, of which it is a sample."[20]

One Biblical passage must suffice to illustrate this tension. In II Corinthians 1:10 Paul says, "who delivered us out of so great a death, and will deliver." The deliverance is both past and future, a present realization and promise for the future.

Would Aristotle say that the divine drama is complete, or if incomplete, that it should run on indefinitely in terms of the present action? He called for a beginning, a middle, and an end. We have traced the drama from its beginning in the creation through the rising action of the middle up to the mid-point, the climax of the great redemptive acts of Calvary and Easter. We have seen the situation of the church

19 T. A. Kantonen, *The Christian Hope* (Muhlenberg, 1945), p. 17.
20 J. H. Yoder, *Peace Without Eschatology?* (Unpublished paper), p. 2.

in the tension of the falling action in this new age when the mid-point lies no longer in the future, but in the past. Must there not be also an end?

We base our argument and our faith, however, not on the analogy of a literary plot, but on the New Testament Scriptures themselves. Surely one cannot read the New Testament without being impressed with the enormous attention paid to things yet to be! "Philemon and III John, each containing only one chapter, are the only books in the New Testament which do not deal with prediction in some fashion . . . every chapter in Matthew, John, Philippians, I Thessalonians, II Timothy, Titus, I Peter, II Peter, II John, Jude, and Revelation, eleven of the twenty-seven books, deals with prediction in some way. Of the 260 chapters of the New Testament, at least 222 have something in them related to Scriptural prediction."[21]

And the things that are said are so very important! "Christian eschatology," says Van Oostersee, "the more the course of time advances, must become less and less an unimportant appendix, and more and more a *locus primarius* [chief center] of Christian doctrine."[22] Emil Brunner urges the same argument: ". . . eschatology is not merely an appendix to Christian doctrine. Rather faith makes no affirmations but such as ever imply the Christian hope of the future. . . . Christian faith is so closely bound up with the Christian hope of the future that faith and hope can be regarded as two aspects of one and the same thing: the revelation of the Christ. . . . The whole content of the Christian faith is oriented towards the *telos*, the end."[23]

21 R. B. Jones, *The Things Which Shall Be Hereafter* (Broadman, 1947), p. 23.

22 Quoted by Geo. H. N. Peters, *Theocratic Kingdom* (Kregel, Grand Rapids, 1952), III, p. 321.

23 Emil Brunner, *Eternal Hope* (Westminster, 1954), p. 28.

That is, the Christian is not merely at liberty to study eschatology if his interests happen to run in that direction. He is under the necessity of bringing in the *eschaton* if he would understand his faith. The minister who never preaches eschatology is preaching a Christianity which is full of loose ends. What some of those loose ends are we propose to show in some detail in the lectures which will follow. In this introduction I trust it has been made clear that there are dramatic and Scriptural reasons why the drama of redemption should go on to a logical end. The plot calls for a denouement, and revelation has given us a great deal of predictive information concerning the final unfolding of the plot. We have come nearly two thousand years from the mid-point of the divine time line. How long that line will be we do not know. But we know it will have an end. It will not stretch out to infinity. Our Alpha will also be our Omega.

II

A BRIEF HISTORY
OF ESCHATOLOGY

Before we go farther into our discussion of the End that must come, let us trace briefly the views on eschatology which have bidden at one time or another for acceptance. Here, as in other areas of Bible truth, there have been various systems of interpretation which have led to very different conclusions. These differences are unfortunate, for they have often led to unchristian attitudes. At the Prophecy Conference in New York in 1953 we were told that in England some pre-tribulationists and post-tribulationists will not sit together on the same platform. Wilbur M. Smith says, "If there is any body of people in this country prone to divide bitterly, it is the students of prophecy."[1]

Another effect of the differences is that some have concluded it is impossible to know anything for sure about eschatology, and so they have discarded this area of truth altogether, to their great loss. The approach to the study of eschatology must always be intensely spiritual; otherwise it is full of danger, as the history of the doctrine abundantly shows. "If . . . our hearts are not primarily interested in the Saviour and Lord whose second coming is the central theme of all eschatology," says Kromminga, "if we carry not with us into such study the living appreciation of His incarna-

[1] Wilbur M. Smith, in preface to George E. Ladd, *Crucial Questions About the Kingdom of God* (Eerdmans, 1952), p. 12.

14

tion and atoning death and glorious resurrection as the eternal Son of God, our danger is . . . great. And if we begin to ask all kinds of questions suggested by human curiosity concerning subjects about which God has not deemed it necessary and wise to give us fuller information than the Bible contains, we shall be tempted to allow the play of our imagination to fill the places which God has left blank. In the eschatological field such vacant places are perhaps more frequent than in any other doctrinal field."[2]

But let us look at the history of eschatology. We have seen that the Old Testament prophets prophesied chiefly in terms of a triumphant kingdom on the earth. Their prophecies by a natural transition developed into apocalyptic, which abounds in dreams, visions, and symbols. Daniel is a book of the Old Testament canon which is a good illustration of this literary type. In the period between the Testaments the apocalyptic method was used in a considerable body of noncanonical writings. It became, as John Bright says, the pathology, the disease, of Judaism. "Forever scanning the times for signs of the coming end, drawing diagrams, as it were, of how that end should come, it moved in a dream world where the coming of the Kingdom was momentarily expected in clouds and glory."[3] At its best, apocalypticism was good. "It believed in a God who worked a purpose in history, it believed that events marched onward toward their appointed end—the triumph of the divine design . . . it was eschatological: it looked for 'last things,' the effective terminus toward which history moves."[4] At its worst it was Jewish phantasy which was chiefly aimed at

2 D. H. Kromminga, *The Millennium in the Church* (Eerdmans, 1945), p. 292.

3 John Bright, *The Kingdom of God* (Abingdon, 1953), p. 168.

4 J. E. Fison, *The Christian Hope* (Longmans, 1954), p. 183.

satisfying curiosity, at giving a peep behind the scenes, and diverted attention from the more serious principles of true prophecy. Yet it was a form which God could use, for one book also of the New Testament canon, Revelation, is in the apocalyptic style. Apocalyptic became popular in a time of severe persecution, when the Jews, and then the Christians, were struggling to exist. It is an index of a real faith in God who would intervene to save His people and to bring His cause to triumph.

Jesus' disciples and the early church were well acquainted with the apocalyptic of the time. The promise of the Lord that He would return was not hard for them to accept. They looked for Him very soon. The early church lived in constant expectation of the Parousia, with all that it would bring of judgment and the completion of the Kingdom. All the apostles taught of the Return, and exhorted to watchful, expectant living, in view of the imminent Parousia. They longed for that event, for while the Jews had looked for a Messiah they did not know, the Christians were now looking for a Lord they knew and loved.

However, the passage of years without the promised Parousia brought new eschatological ideas to the post-New Testament era. Based no doubt in part upon the mention in Revelation 20 of a thousand-year reign of Christ, but combined with Jewish apocalyptic, chiliasm came upon the scene. Chiliasm held that Christ would return to reign in Jerusalem for a thousand years before the final judgment. ". . . Till the beginning of the fifth century A.D., chiliasm . . . was extensively found within the Christian Church, but . . . never was dominant, far less universal, . . . it was not without opponents, and . . . its representatives were conscious of being able to speak only for a party in the church. . . . Chiliasm never found creedal expression or approbation in the ancient church," says Kromminga.[5] The chiliasts believed that the Kingdom must find its earthly as well as its heavenly perfection. But their enthusiastic hopes led them to some very extravagant descriptions. For instance, Papias says, "The days shall come, in which vines shall grow, each having ten thousand shoots, and on each shoot ten thousand branches, and on each branch again ten thousand twigs, and on each twig ten thousand clusters, and on each cluster ten thousand grapes, and each grape when pressed shall yield five-and-twenty measures of wine. And when any of the saints shall have taken hold of one of their clusters, another shall say, I am a better cluster; take me, bless the Lord through me. Likewise also a grain of wheat shall produce ten thousand heads, and every head shall have ten thousand grains and every grain ten pounds of fine flour, bright and clean, and the other fruits, seeds, and the grass shall produce in similar proportions, and all the animals using these fruits which are products of the soil, shall become in their turn peaceable and harmonious, obedient to man in all subjection."[6]

Augustine, who lived about A.D. 400, was repelled by the material ideas of the early chiliasts. In his *City of God* he set up the theory which was to be dominant in Christendom for almost 1500 years. He taught that the church is the Kingdom, and that the age of the church between Pentecost and Christ's coming in judgment is the millennium, the thousand-year reign of Christ. He expected the constant growth and the gradual success of the church in overcoming all evil before the return of the Lord. This is called postmillennialism. From this system of thought grew the con-

---

5 D. H. Kromminga, *op. cit.,* p. 51.
6 Quoted by W. H. Rutgers, *Premillennialism in America* (Goes, 1930), pp. 56 f.

cept of the *corpus christianum,* a whole social order, including the state, brought under the Lordship of Christ. There
has been an evangelical postmillennialism which, as J. C.
Wenger points out, "held that before the return of Jesus and
before the end of the world . . . peace and righteousness
would prevail on earth through the spread of the church
and the effective ministry of the Gospel and the blessed work
of the Holy Spirit."[7] There has also been the liberal expression of postmillennialism which expected to bring in the
Kingdom by reform, and eliminated the whole concept of
a Parousia. Case gave expression to this point of view in
these words: "Evils still unconquered are to be eliminated
by strenuous efforts and gradual reform, rather than by the
catastrophic intervention of Deity."[8] The postmillennial interpretation shows the Greek influence, the development of
history by cycles rather than by crises of intervention by the
Divine. The tendency of this approach is to place such emphasis on what man can do to "bring in the Kingdom" as to
make less necessary the catastrophic or climactic act of God
in a second coming of Christ. The kingdom on earth looms
so large that the heavenly Kingdom, the Kingdom which
God, not man, sets up, tends to fall into the shadows. For
medieval times the Kingdom of God was the church, but the
church was more like a state than a church.

The Reformation brought eschatology into a new focus
of interest again. Torrance describes this: ". . . the Reformation stands for the rediscovery of the living God of the Bible, who actively intervenes in the affairs of men . . . and
with that comes a powerful realization of the historical perspective of Biblical eschatology which envisages both a new
heaven and a new earth . . . the fullness of the creation . . .

7 J. C. Wenger, *Introduction to Theology* (Herald Press, 1954), p. 36.
8 Shirley Jackson Case, *The Millennial Hope* (Univ. of Chicago Press,
1919), p. 229.

unimpaired in union with a heavenly consummation."[9] But the reformers, clinging to the idea of the *corpus christianum* in the state church, failed to return to the New Testament understanding of the church as the pilgrim people of God. The church was still very well domesticated in the world in which it was at home, and so eschatology for many of the reformers had an academic rather than a real and present interest.

Not so with the more thorough reformers, the Anabaptists. Two expressions of their eschatology are of special interest. The main stream of the Anabaptists, setting out to restore within the fellowship of the brotherhood the true spiritual principles of Christ as taught in the New Testament, ran foul of the determined intention of the state churches and became the victims of bitter persecution. In their sufferings they gave expression to an eschatology of martyrdom. It was not a charted system, nor did it attempt to describe a future triumph in the Kingdom of God. The martyrs only knew that their martyrdoms were the result of the struggle of Antichrist against Christ. ". . . the old dragon . . . rages with doubled ferocity, and the prayers of the martyred saints rise up to heaven until the number of these martyrs shall be full."[10] Then the tables will be turned, "the day of retaliation will dawn, a day of glory for the martyrs, and a day of horror for the persecutors."[11] "The thought of a speedy and just vindication strengthens the believers to bear the terror of the persecutions."[12] There is comfort in the assurance of final victory when "they shall look on him

9 T. F. Torrance, "The Eschatology of the Reformation," in *Eschatology* (Oliver and Boyd, Edinburgh, 1952).

10 Ethelbert Stauffer, "Theology of Martyrdom," *Mennonite Quarterly Review*, July, 1945.

11 *Ibid.*

12 Orley Swartzentruber, "Theology of Martyrs' Mirror," *Mennonite Quarterly Review*, January, 1954.

whom they have pierced." The Christ whom the martyrs followed in this way of suffering was more real to them than anything in the present world.

In a fringe of fanatical Anabaptists there is a recurrence of the chiliasm of the early centuries. But these wild enthusiasts, going beyond the first chiliasts, were no longer willing to wait for Christ to come and set up His throne. The radical Münsterites attempted by force to restore a kingdom which was more Jewish than Christian. Hofmann set the date when the New Jerusalem was to be established at Strasbourg. These foolish ideas, however, were quickly proved in error, and although they have often been taken as typical of the Anabaptists, were found only in a radical fringe.

The religion of humanism which grew up after the Renaissance caused a fading out of the eschatological hope. The religion of Man has no need for hope in God. The doctrine of evolution, which came on in time, gave man a substitute hope in what he might be able to do in evolving better men and a better social order. This dominant philosophy in the world deeply affected theology and Christian thought. Church history since the Reformation is the story of the gradual elimination of eschatology. Recoiling from the apocalypticism of the Anabaptist fringe, the Reformers kept eschatology in their creeds but cut it loose from their philosophy of history and their teaching. "The eschatological scheme of the New Testament . . . has been silently dropped from recent doctrinal discussion. . . . There has been a progressive detachment of all Christian doctrine, including that of the Last Things, from its original eschatological framework."[13] The age of science made Biblical es-

13 J. A. T. Robinson, *In the End God* (J. Clark and Son, London, 1952), p. 11.

chatology seem like a fairy tale. And modern man could
not reject science! And so by 1873 an article in the *Westminster Review* could call the Second Advent of Christ an
"exploded superstition."[14] "The whole New Testament
prospect of a return of Christ accompanied by the transformation of this world-order, a general resurrection, a final
judgment, and the vindication of the sovereignty of God
over heaven and earth, is regarded by the scientific humanist
of the twentieth century as frankly fantastic. . . . The Second Advent and its accompaniments appear to the modern
man as a simple contradiction of all his presumptions about
the future of the world, immediate or remote. . . . For contemporary thought today the Christian doctrine of the Last
Things is dead, and no one has even bothered to bury it."[15]

When the World Council of Churches announced "Christ
the Hope of the World" as its main theme at the Second
Assembly at Evanston, and it became apparent that this
would involve eschatology, many churchmen were embar-
rassed to have to discuss a doctrine in which they did not
believe. Their eschatology had become completely secular-
ized by the philosophy of progress and the gospel of world
change by social action. "Liberal Christianity," says Williams, "had faith that the world can be moved. The kingdom, it believed, is coming in history. World bettering is
Kingdom-building. He who shares in that work knows that
his life is linked with the purpose of God. Every victory of
righteousness moves the whole creation toward its consummation in the everlasting community of love."[16] That this
attitude has characterized much foreign mission work is
seen in the fact, for instance, that in the eighty years of Prot-

---

14 Geo. H. N. Peters, *Theocratic Kingdom* (Kregel, 1952), p. 164.
15 J. A. T. Robinson, *op. cit.*, p. 15.
16 D. D. Williams, *God's Grace and Man's Hope* (Harper, 1949), p. 83.

estant Christianity in Japan, the main emphasis has been on the ethical and social aspects of the Christian message, and in the recently expressed need of Japanese Christians for "more of the . . . eschatological."[17]

A frank statement of the current attitude of liberals in America was given by R. L. Calhoun in an address at Evanston: ". . . our theology has come to lay especial stress on ethics and to be far less confident about eschatology. . . . Its hope has been centered in the manifest power of God to overcome evil with good here and now, and throughout man's future on earth. It does not forget the final judgment nor the life everlasting, but its chief confidence has been in God's grace from day to day, and its chief stress on the duty of every Christian to live as a devoted follower and servant of Jesus Christ. . . . The Christian Gospel is a word for this world . . . not a remote ideal nor a way of escape."[18]

Biblical eschatology did not, however, fall into complete forgetfulness just because the church as a whole neglected it. Throughout the Protestant era there have been able and faithful teachers of the Christian Hope. There were evangelical postmillennialists who expected the Parousia, even though their system of thought, it seems to us, does not accord with New Testament teaching of a struggle between God and His enemies to the very end. There were nonmillennialists, or amillennialists, who though they did not expect Christ to set up a world-embracing Kingdom at all, did believe devoutly that He would return to bring time to an end and to inaugurate the eternal ages by a resurrection and a judgment. And there were scholarly and devout premillennialists, who rejected many of the extravagances of

17 Darley Downs, *Christian Century*, March 3, 1954.
18 R. L. Calhoun, "Christ the Hope of the World," *Christian Century*, Aug. 25, 1954.

chiliasm and yet taught that Christ would return to set up a reign on earth. Reese mentions the following great Bible teachers, among others, who were such premillennialists: Alford, Bonar, Erdman, Gordon, Saphir, Tregelles, Trench, West, Delitzsch, Godet, Lange, Meyer.[19] These "historical premillennialists," with some differences of detail, no doubt, expected the visible, personal advent of Christ. The Parousia was an event, a crisis, accompanied by the resurrection of the dead in Christ, the translation of living saints, the destruction of the Antichrist, the repentance of Israel. Then would come the thousand-year reign of Christ, followed by the completion of resurrection, the Last Judgment, and the creation of the eternal world. The essential feature of premillennialism was "the concept of a parenthesis time period" between the Parousia and the eternal state.[20]

We can be thankful for the lovers of the Appearing who kept alive a reverent and believing study of the prophetic Scriptures. These, says Minear, "have preserved an awareness of God's transcendence over the world of time and space, a conviction that there will be a real vindication of God's justice achieved by His power rather than by human strategy, a stubborn refusal to surrender the future to any other Lord than Jesus Christ, and a readiness to live in this world as pilgrims and strangers. That these basic convictions have been identified with fanciful speculations and clouded over with ethical absurdities has been in part due to an understandable aversion to the excesses of a modernism that has confused Christian hope with humanistic eschatology."[21]

19 Alexander Reese, *The Approaching Advent of Christ* (Marshall, Morgan, and Scott, 1937), p. 18.

20 C. Norman Kraus, *Dispensationalism—Rise and Development* (Unpublished thesis), p. 107.

21 Paul S. Minear, *Christian Hope and the Second Coming* (Westminster, 1954), p. 86.

A very unfortunate result of the prevalent neglect of eschatology was the rash of extremist apocalyptic systems which broke out while the main line theologians were keeping silence. In its Second Report the Advisory Commission of the World Council of Churches wrote in 1952: ". . . one reason for the rise of extreme . . . beliefs is the virtual disappearance . . . in the preaching of many churches of the distinctly Christian hopes in Christ's coming again. Those who preach apocalyptic views are right in pointing out that the New Testament is full of references to a salvation yet to be revealed, a Kingdom yet to come. The response which they evoke among many who are poor, wretched, and despised or disillusioned and frustrated is a reminder to us that many hearts long for some mighty change in things as they are, some great deliverance from their lot."[22]

These apocalyptic sects have risen in great numbers, not only in Europe and America, but on the mission fields as well. We mention only three: Seventh-Day Adventism, Jehovah's Witnesses, and Dispensationalism. The first two have gained an enormous world-wide following. But we will describe only the third, because "it has become a major force in modern American Protestantism."[23]

Dispensationalism was developed following 1830 by J. N. Darby and others. This theory was widely taught in both England and America through lecture tours, Bible conferences, books, Bible institutes, and a special edition of the Bible with notes by C. I. Scofield. Dispensationalism was premillennial. But it added to historical premillennialism certain details which had not been taught before. Jesus' coming was divided into two stages: the secret "rapture,"

22 *Second Report of the Advisory Commission,* World Council of Churches (New York, 1952), p. 3.
23 H. S. Bender, "History of Millennial Theories," *Prophecy Conference* (Herald Press, 1953), p. 49.

when the saved, both the dead and the living, would be caught up to meet the Lord who had come *for* them; and the "revelation," seven years later, when the Lord would come *with* His saints to destroy His enemies and set up His Kingdom. During the seven years, said to be Daniel's seventieth week, would occur the Great Tribulation, with the Antichrist in full power. This Antichrist was to be destroyed at the Battle of Armageddon when Christ would come in avenging might. An important feature in Dispensationalism was the separation of all history into seven periods, or "dispensations," each with a different principle of administration. We are now, according to this scheme, in the sixth, the dispensation of grace. When Christ came the first time He intended to set up His Kingdom, the final dispensation. But when the Jew rejected Him, the Kingdom was "postponed," and the Church Age, the dispensation of grace, became an unannounced "parenthesis" between the Dispensation of Law and the Kingdom Age. Old Testament prophecies and "Kingdom teachings" of the New Testament were to be applied, not to the church, but to the millennial Kingdom. In the literature of the movement this was called "rightly dividing the word of truth." Lewis Sperry Chafer, the chief theologian of dispensationalism, says, "The Scriptures addressed to [Christians] are: the Gospel by John—especially the Upper Room Discourse, the Acts, and the Epistles."[24] In the millennium the Jews would be the center of interest. They are to have turned to the Lord at the Revelation, and the millennium is to be their restored Kingdom, with Christ ruling them from Jerusalem. The church and the Jews have separate eschatologies, says Chafer, reaching separately into eternity.[25]

24 *Dispensationalism* (Dallas Seminary Press, 1951), p. 34.
25 *Op. cit.*, p. 65.

One example of where dispensational thinking takes one must suffice. Peters, author an of exhaustive three-volume work on dispensationalism, writes concerning the use of the sword in the millennium: "The writer has no sympathy with Romanists [and] some Protestants . . . that saints and believers now, under the present ordering, are to take the sword to advance the truth for the church, or the cause of Christ. This is positively forbidden; and, therefore, we must await *the time and the ordering* appointed by God Himself. The quotation so common among the Puritans, 'that the saints should have the praises of God in their mouths, and a two-edged sword in their hands,' was in that day and time a misapplication of Scripture. . . . Predictions wholly relating to the future, are wrongly misappropriated . . . if priests, ministers, popes, and kings misapplied them in their self-interest, that is no reason why we should reject them, and refuse them an *ultimate realization*."[26]

It should be emphasized that historic premillennialism and dispensationalism are not synonymous. As Bear has pointed out, "Both believed in a Kingdom of Christ on earth after His return. But the historic premillennialist exalted the church and held that the church enjoyed the Kingdom. If the Jews were to have any place of pre-eminence, it was because they had become a part of the church. [Dispensationalists] make the Kingdom a Jewish Kingdom, given to the Jews because they are Jews. The church has become a special group, different in character and destiny . . . ."[27] And Reese, a premillennialist, says, "Premillennialism never had a greater millstone round its neck than the mass of vagaries that [Darbyism] propounds."[28]

26 Geo. H. N. Peters, *op. cit.,* II, pp. 103 f.
27 James E. Bear, "Historic Premillennialism," *Union Seminary Review* (Richmond), May, 1944, quoted by Kraus, *op. cit.,* p. 87.
28 Alexander Reese, *op. cit.,* p. 295.

Another effect of the neglect of Scriptural eschatology is the encouragement of secular eschatologies. ". . . the history of our time testifies that if religion does not furnish men with a hope [for the future,] they will very soon devise secular substitutes for it. (We think of Hitler's dream of a *Reich* which would last a thousand years, Mussolini's vision of a new and greater Roman empire, and Soviet Russia's myth of a class-less society after the final 'showdown' between capitalism and communism.)"[29] Marx, the father of communist thinking, had a Judeo-Christian background. But he eliminated God in favor of materialism. For the hope of a divine Kingdom he substituted a hope in a revolution which would eliminate the capitalists. His millennium was the Communist Commonwealth. Communism has all the enthusiasm of a religious faith. One reason it is such a threat is the intense enthusiasm with which communists hold to their credo and their hope of a better world to come. Communism might not have been born if Marx had seen a real hope in the Christian Church of his day. The best way to meet communism in our world is to confront it with a better eschatology, with a confident faith in the promises which God has made.[30]

The sleep of the theologians concerning eschatology had an awakening at the turn of the twentieth century through the writing of Albert Schweitzer, who contended that the New Testament, both the sayings of Jesus and the writings of the apostles, was radically eschatological. Schweitzer taught that Jesus expected to return soon, within a few years, to establish His Kingdom. He challenged the liberalism which thought it could easily eliminate eschatology from the Gospel, and in that he did a great service. But

29 Archibald M. Hunter, "The Hope of Glory," *Interpretation*, April, 1954.
30 J. E. Fison, *op. cit.*, p. 54.

his dismissing Jesus as a "heroic but misguided fanatic" is not, of course, in the interests of a true expectation of Christ.

Another step in bringing back eschatology to theological circles was the "realized eschatology" of C. H. Dodd and others. This group recognized the large eschatological element in the New Testament but held that it was all realized in the first coming of Christ. This school of thought has done a service in emphasizing the importance of what Christ has already done, in developing more clearly the meaning of the climax. No doubt the sects on one hand and Schweitzer on the other had developed an eschatological fever, a preoccupation with the future. But realized eschatology makes the opposite error of neglecting the large number of statements "whose thrust was obviously futuristic."[31] Dodd has left us, says Fison, "in a situation in which everything that really matters has happened already. This is to destroy the original meaning of *eschaton* altogether."[32]

We are living today in a time of great interest in eschatology, more so than any time since the Reformation. Sects with unorthodox eschatologies continue to grow. But in the main line churches too the subject has increasing attention. The World Council of Churches found this the logical choice for the main theme at Evanston. The discussions there brought the Second Coming of Christ to the attention of many who had never heard much about it before, and the publicity of that meeting put the subject on front pages. Scores of books and magazine articles on eschatology have been written recently, and several lectureships other than this one have chosen this area of Christian thought.

31 Harold B. Kuhn, "Contemporary Thought on the Christian Hope," *United Evangelical Action*, May 15, 1954.
32 *Op. cit.*, p. 88.

Joseph Sitler, a Lutheran theologian, wrote in a Chicago newspaper at the time of the Evanston Assembly: "Modern Biblical studies are in a period of great creative reformation. With great clarity and force the rich and many-dimensioned character of the Biblical teaching about man's hope in Christ is being rediscovered. . . ."[33]

Paul Minear has written, "A far-reaching revolution is under way, spurred on by a world-wide revival of Biblical theology, and spearheaded by a new respect for Biblical eschatology."[34] And John Howard Yoder says, "After the breakdown of optimistic liberalism, dogmatics is returning to an appreciation of the importance of the eschatological dimension in Christian faith."[35]

One cause for this renewed interest in a future hope is the mounting tragedy in our chaotic world. Martin Niemoeller has fittingly studied *Revelation* with Christians living under the communist tyranny in East Germany. The progress of our civilization fails to impress war victims who live in cellars and concentration camps. The whole concept of gradually building the Kingdom "has foundered on the rocks not so much of human sin, as of the contradictions and complexities of the very western culture which was the substance of . . . belief."[36] And Reinhold Niebuhr says, "We are living in an age in which the modern substitute for Christian eschatology, which was once so plausible, has become more fantastic than the Christian hope of the Parousia of Christ."[37]

33 Chicago *Sun-Times,* Aug. 27, 1954.

34 *Op. cit.,* p. 88.

35 Review of Herbert Butterfield's *Christianity, Diplomacy, and War, Mennonite Quarterly Review,* July, 1954.

36 David M. Paton, *Christian Missions and the Judgment of God* (S.C.M. Press, 1953), p. 28.

37 Reinhold Niebuhr, "Christ the Hope of the World," *Religion in Life,* Summer, 1954.

Certainly much of this new eschatological interest is not resting as it should upon the firm foundation of revelation. There are many attempts to demythologize the Biblical prophecies to meet the demands of modern science. But on the whole we can rejoice in a willingness to consider again matters that had once been called exploded myths. The student of prophecy today is not limited to the charts and diagrams of dispensationalists.

Certainly it is a matter for which we can be profoundly grateful that eschatology is coming into its rightful place in theology. It is not an appendix, but must infuse and permeate all Biblical studies. ". . . everything in Christian theology turns on the real presence of One who is really God and really in history."[38] Paul Peachey has well expressed the need, not only of the individual Christian, but also of the church, for a better understanding of eschatology: "There needs to be a recovery of eschatological comprehension. . . . We need to understand anew the ways of God in history. True, men have failed, but even in the midst of that failure the Kingdom of God is moving toward fulfillment. Excessive preoccupation with attempts to read the signs of the times regarding future events cannot but dim our understanding of the here and now. Unhealthy speculation about the eschatological calendar can even be a way to bury the talent He has given us. On the other hand, we need desperately a recovery of genuine eschatological expectancy of the secret of the true saints of all ages who have awaited the aeon to come because they were already in it and whose future was illuminated as much by their present possession as was their present experience by their hope of future glory."[39]

38 W. H. Whitehouse, "The Modern Discussion of Eschatology" (Oliver & Boyd, 1952), p. 72.

39 "Toward an Understanding of the Decline of the West," *Concern*, June, 1954, pp. 43 f.

As God's creatures, we have had a beginning in His creation. As His children we have been made His by the work of Christ in the fullness, the climax of time. Growing up to maturity in Him, seeking to find meaning in our *own* lives and in the history of the world, we must understand the End toward which all things move.

III

FINDING CERTAINTY
IN ESCHATOLOGY

We have seen that the drama of redemption which God has revealed to us in the Scriptures has, like every drama, a beginning, a middle, and an end. We traced that drama from its beginning in the creation to the mid-point, the climax of Christ's coming to redeem us by His death and resurrection. We saw that Christ at that time brought in the New Age, in which His work in and for us is being blessedly realized. But we also saw that His work needs to go on to a completion not yet realized. We live in a tension between that which we have already received and that which we look forward to with hope. We live in the times of the End, but we have not yet come to the End. The drama is not yet complete, but some day, according to the Scriptures, it will be. Christ our Alpha will become also Christ our Omega.

We have also traced the development of eschatological ideas from Old Testament times to our own day. We took notice of different schools of interpretation. We saw that there were periods of low interest and of high interest in eschatological studies, and rejoiced to observe that we are at present in a peak period of interest in the Christian Hope.

We must now consider in greater detail some lines of action in the drama which are not complete and which cannot be completed without the promised Parousia and the End of time. Before we do this, however, we must give some attention to the basis of our belief in this promised End. How do we find certainty concerning events yet future? In a field in which there are great differences of opinion and understanding, how can one find any firm ground on which to stand?

The first thing to be said in answer to these questions is that the Bible is our only source of information about the future. We can urge by logic that all the past calls for a future, and a future that brings a logical end. But that is only logic. The honest truth is that only God knows the future. We can know it only as He reveals it. This He has done in the Bible. Through Old Testament prophets He forecast the shape of things to come. The marvelous way in which many of these forecasts became history in the first coming of Christ gives us confidence that those prophecies still unfulfilled, as well as the predictions of our Lord as recorded in the Gospels and of the apostles in the other books of the New Testament canon, will likewise become events in a real historic sense. Anyone who believes in the deity of Christ and in the inspiration of the Scriptures cannot think otherwise. All eschatology is definitely based on the revealed purpose and promise of God. The Waldensians have given us their "Noble Lesson": "The Scriptures speak, and we must believe. Look at the Scriptures from beginning to end."[1]

Obviously this confidence in the promise has back of it a confidence in the God who promised. Paul preached a certain hope because "God, who never lies, promised [it] ages ago."[2] The character of God is back of what He says.

1 Quoted by Geo. H. N. Peters, *The Theocratic Kingdom* (Kregel, Grand Rapids, 1952), I, p. 112.
2 Titus 1:2 (Williams).

He will not promise what He is not able to perform. Of this we can be "absolutely certain."[3] Saints of old, like Abraham, "did not in unbelief hesitate about God's promise,"[4] and neither need we. "He is faithful that promised"[5] —both able and faithful. Any failure, then, to believe the divine promise of prophecy impugns the character of God.

That answer, then, that we know about the future because God has told us, seems very simple. This should be the end of the matter. But there is a further question: What does the promise mean? There are often problems in the understanding of language. It is the weakness, not of prophecy, but of prophecy students, that they read their own meanings into the Word. Oftentimes where the Word is silent they try to fill in the blanks. And so we have the rash of prophetic blueprints which has brought all eschatology into a disrepute which it does not deserve. Brunner complains that "we possess dozens or hundreds of . . . doctrinal schemes claiming to delineate the end of the world, and to follow precisely Holy Scripture, yet all mutually contradictory. . . ."[6]

The student of Biblical prophecy has no call to become a prophet. "Revelation is enough. Speculation is more than enough."[7] Kantonen gives us good counsel: ". . . when the Word is silent we dare not speak. The Word does indeed manifest throughout a spirit of chaste caution which serves to check our natural curiosity and imagination. Ideas . . . speculation . . . mystical flights . . . —these must be recognized as such and clearly distinguished from true Christian eschatology."[8] We must not be afraid to admit

3 Rom. 4:21 (Weymouth).
4 Rom. 4:20 (Berkeley).
5 Heb. 10:23.
6 Emil Brunner, *Eternal Hope* (Westminster, 1954), p. 185.
7 Geo. P. Eckman, *When Christ Comes Again* (Abingdon, 1917), p. 21.
8 T. A. Kantonen, *The Christian Hope* (Muhlenberg, 1954), p. 3.

that there are many things we do not know. Blanks must remain blank. Wild long ago said, "I charge you to beware of prophetic dentists who put false teeth in the mouth of prophecy."[9]

But we may make serious errors also in the interpretation of what is written. There is great danger that we will adopt a system or point of view and then bend every Scripture to make it fit our plan. It is an elementary rule of exegesis, says Reese, "that we must not introduce our ideas into the text, but draw the natural and obvious meaning from it."[10] To do this requires not only ability in reading the Scriptures, but utmost honesty which will be willing to accept what the Scripture clearly says, even if it runs counter to our earlier ideas. It is not important that our system be defended; it is important that the Word of God be heard.

The language of eschatology, we must be free to admit, offers difficulties. There is large use of imagery and symbolism which requires interpretation. Peter J. Twisk, a Mennonite who lived about 1600, wrote in *The Peaceful Kingdom of Christ,* "For that in a natural sense every hill shall be made low, and every valley shall be exalted, I hope no one who with half an eye reads the Bible believes and as this one thing is not to be understood in a natural sense, so are also other prophecies and figurative declarations of God's Word not to be taken as though it would occur . . . in a natural sense."[11] It is difficult to find an accurate translation of words and ideas, as in the case of Parousia. The otherworldly concepts of eschatology can scarcely be contained in our mundane speech. Revelation is partial; that

9 Quoted by Peters, *op. cit.,* III, p. 274.
10 Alexander Reese, *The Approaching Advent of Christ* (Marshall, Morgan, and Scott, 1937), pp. 200 f.
11 Peter J. Twisk, *The Peaceful Kingdom of Christ* (Elkhart, 1913), pp. 11 f.

is, not all prophetic truth is collected in one place and arranged in an orderly sequence. There is required much comparing of texts. Even then there will seem to be contradictions. These must be considered in the light of the entire body of truth. The doubtful must be interpreted by the plainly revealed.[12] In eschatology we are trying to understand historical developments in which we ourselves are involved, and it is difficult to secure perspective. The present moment always seems, somehow, to be of tremendous importance. The prophetic Word, because it is so universal, seems to speak particularly to our own time. Jaspers warns us, ". . . it . . . remains impossible for us to judge an historical phenomenon *in toto* and definitively. For we are not the Deity, who sits in judgment, but men, who open their senses in order to gain a share in the historical."[13]

The Bible wants to be its own interpreter. Any phrase or sentence must be allowed to say what it means in its own immediate or larger context. Passages pulled out of their historical and literary setting may be made to say almost anything. There is a kind of literal interpretation which can do great violence to the truth. Says Kantonen: "But neither can we simply compile all the passages in which the Bible speaks of the last things and then proceed to construct our own mosaic. It is this kind of uncritical and static Biblicism that is responsible for the existing variety of contradictory . . . eschatologies . . . a sound concept of the Word is indispensable. Eschatology must be in harmony with the living center of the Word, God's revelation of Himself in Christ. Obscure passages must be interpreted in the light of the clear and unmistakable truth of the Gospel. The visions, ecstasies, and symbols . . . must be related to

12 Peters, *op. cit.*, II, p. 512.
13 Karl Jaspers, *The Origin and Goal of History* (Yale, 1953), p. 234.

the basic and unquestionable affirmations of faith and not used to set them aside."[14]

Two methods of interpretation, the "literal" and the "spiritual," are often spoken of as being opposed to one another. The literal is the plain meaning which lies on the surface. Much of the Bible may be interpreted in this way. Cooper's rule has often been quoted: "When the plain sense of Scripture makes common sense, seek no other sense; therefore take every word at its primary, ordinary, usual, literary meaning unless the facts of the context indicate clearly otherwise."[15] Spiritual interpretation is supposed to look for spiritual, perhaps allegorical, meaning behind the plain sense of the words. But as R. B. Jones observes, "the names are not altogether fortunate. The words 'literal' and 'spiritual' are not antonyms, strictly speaking. 'Literal' applies to language and is the antonym of 'figurative' or 'symbolic.' 'Spiritual' has to do with the realm of application and is the antonym of 'natural' or 'material.' Literal language may have fulfillment in the spiritual realm, just as figurative language may find its application in the material realm; and both realms—the material and the spiritual—are real."[16]

The way in which the New Testament writers interpret the Old Testament prophecies is of special importance for us as a guide to getting at the true meaning of the predictive Scriptures. For the New Testament writers were inspired to interpret the inspired Old Testament Scriptures. The interpretations of modern commentators may be, and often obviously are, erroneous. The interpreters are fallible. But the New Testament interpreters are infallible, the only infallible interpreters which we have to depend upon. Ols-

14 *Op. cit.*, p. 3.
15 David Cooper, quoted by R. B. Jones, *The Things Which Shall Be Hereafter* (Broadman, 1947), p. 6.
16 *Ibid.*, p. 6.

hausen says, "The explanation of the Old Testament in
the New is the very point from which alone all explanation
that listens to the voice of divine wisdom must set out. For
we have here presented to us the sense of Holy Scripture
as understood by inspired men themselves, and are furnished
with the true key of knowledge."[17]

These inspired interpreters often interpreted literally,
particularly in prophecies such as the birth at Bethlehem
which helped to identify Jesus as the promised Messiah.
But they also interpreted figuratively when they saw fulfilled in Christ's life and work some Old Testament prophecy that was in physical language. For instance, Peter at
Pentecost explains what has happened as a fulfillment of
a prophecy: ". . . this is that which hath been spoken
through the prophet Joel." He does not hesitate because
Joel spoke of physical accompaniments which were not seen
at Pentecost. He took the heart of the prophecy and saw its
fulfillment in the experience of Spirit baptism. "The Infallible Interpreters," says Jones, "have blazed a trail for
us. Their teachings clearly indicate the place of both the
literal and the symbolic principles of interpretation. And
they show us that spiritual applications become more and
more important as the fullness of the purposes of grace are
realized."[18]

So then we do not want that misuse of language which by
allegorizing and demythologizing explains away any legiti-
mate meaning of the words. This, says one, "can never be
properly termed interpretation, but . . . only mutilation."[19]
But neither do we want a slavish literalism, such, for instance, as might argue that since Christ is coming in the
clouds, He could not come on some certain cloudless day!

17 Quoted by R. B. Jones, *op. cit.*, p. 17.
18 *Ibid.*, p. 63.
19 Emil Brunner, *op. cit.*, p. 119.

We do want to enter so fully into God's purposes as revealed in the Scriptures that we may, to a degree, "elevate ourselves up to the mind and intention of the Spirit of revelation, and see His whole design. . . ."[20] We want ever to keep our minds open for new light from the Scripture, hoping always to correct any mistaken idea and to deepen the understanding we have already gained. We want to keep ourselves so detached from systems of interpretation as to make sure that prejudice will not blind us to the truth. We want to build our faith on our certainties, not our ignorance. And we want to keep a warm love for our brethren, so that differences of understanding need not disturb our fellowship. We must be more anxious to learn from one another than to refute one another's errors. The delegates at Evanston said, ". . . we saw our differences . . . become diverse insights. . . ."[21]

Let special emphasis rest on the need for humility. We need not sacrifice our convictions. There are some things in eschatology about which we can be positive, even dogmatic. Charles Erdman asserts that "as to the two or three great cardinal facts of prophecy, all . . . schools agree."[22] But because there are gaps in our knowledge through revelation, because we must interpret and harmonize many of the details given us, because the descriptive details given are actually so meager, we do well to keep in mind our limitations. Of the "final development the Holy Scripture speaks only in great, general, basic lines," says Sauer. "It does not impart to us the more exact details. Our curiosity shall not be satisfied, but our hope and sanctification shall

---

20 A. B. Davidson, *Old Testament Prophecy* (T. and T. Clark, Edinburgh, 1912), p. 15.

21 "Statement on Main Theme," *Christian Century*, Sept. 22, 1954.

22 Charles Erdman, *The Return of Christ* (Doran, 1922), p. 72.

ever receive fresh, living, heavenly impulse."[23] Of those great basic lines there need be no argument, for on them the teaching is clear and decisive. And certainly Reese was right in feeling that "It would be fortunate if Christians could reach agreement on a few leading aspects of the Second Coming, instead of stirring up disunity by prophetic speculations on many others that call for patience and tolerance."[24]

In the heavenly kingdom, we are persuaded, there will be found representatives of different schools of interpretation. Their salvation will not be effected by their interpretation, but by their Lord. No doubt they will all have some surprises about reality in comparison with their surmises. They will see then how difficult it is for mortals to comprehend eternal things. Karl Heim says that "when we the children of time try to speak about the realm beyond time, it is as though infants sought to participate in the conversation of adults."[25]

Even on this side of the End further studies may cast further light on the Scriptures, and world events may explain what was before enigma. Christian apologists do not need to have all the answers; they can let some problems wait for solution. "Our wisdom is to 'hold fast that which is good' even though we may be unable to give a completely satisfying account of it."[26]

A proper humility, then, will help the student of eschatology to frankly admit his limits. "It is unwise for Christians to claim any knowledge of either the furniture of

---

23 Erich Sauer, *From Eternity to Eternity* (Eerdmans, 1954), p. 137.

24 Alexander Reese, *op. cit.*, pp. XIII f.

25 Indirect quotation by J. A. Kantonen, *op. cit.*, p. 28.

26 T. F. Glasson, *His Appearing and His Kingdom* (Epworth Press, London, 1953), p. 27.

heaven or the temperature of hell."[27] Humility will also give a healthy tolerance for the opinions of others. " 'Think and let think' was John Wesley's admonition, and it is an admirable precept respecting all matters which are not essential to salvation and the progress of Christ's kingdom."[28] And humility puts a person in position to keep on learning. Dean Alford writes like both a Christian and a scholar when he says, "I think it proper to state in this third edition that having now entered upon the deeper study of the New Testament, I do not feel by any means that full confidence which I once did in the exegesis here given of the three portions of this Chapter twenty-five [Matthew]. . . . I very much question whether the thorough study of Scripture will not make me more and more distrustful of all human systemizing and less willing to hazard assertion on any portion of the subject."[29]

Is there certainty, then, concerning the future scenes of the drama of the ages? Yes, where God has clearly revealed the truth. What about those things that are not clearly revealed? We base our hope on what we know, and where we are ignorant we wait for more light. What is revealed is enough for our present need of a certain hope.

27 Reinhold Niebuhr, *The Nature and Destiny of Man* (Scribners, 1948), II, p. 304.

28 Geo. P. Eckman, *op. cit.*, p. 211.

29 Quoted by George L. Murray, *Millennial Studies* (Baker, 1948), p. 188.

PART II

CHRIST MUST COME AGAIN

IV

CHRIST MUST RETURN
TO COMPLETE HIS WORK

With a prayer that we may hold our certain hope with a humble spirit, we proceed now to a discussion of the need for an eschatological denouement. We shall need to be positive in our conviction that the divine drama must have an end. In this we shall not be seriously contradicted, for there is a reawakened consciousness among Bible students that the New Testament points clearly to a coming End. Any competent interpreter can see that. It takes mutilation not to see it. But it will require reserve and moderation not to overstate our case, not to go beyond the clear meaning of the inspired Word.

Let us begin with the need for Christ to come back to complete His work among men. This is a good place to begin, because it relates the Second Coming to the First Coming. Any prophetic scheme which does not recognize the climactic character of the First Coming is un-Biblical. When preoccupation with the Second Coming makes it the great climax, and the First Coming only a stage toward the climax, the perspective of the New Testament has been lost. The Incarnation did not have as its primary purpose to prepare for the Parousia. On the contrary, the Parousia will occur to bring to completion what was set in motion by the Incarnation. Anything which minimizes the mighty acts which Christ wrought at the mid-point of redemptive history rejects the atoning death and the life-giving resurrection. The center of history is the cross. "The center of Christianity is the faith that the eternal world has broken into time in Jesus as the Christ."[1] It was the First Advent which gives meaning and significance to the Second Advent. We know who is coming and look forward with joy toward that meeting because He was here before, and we have learned to know Him. It is His personality as we have become acquainted with Him in the Gospels that gives content to the future hope. If Christ were only one of many characters to play a part in the future denouement, if He were one to whom something is being done, the End would have a very different character. But He is the one who is doing it! He is the Coming One! We are not looking for something; we are looking for Someone we know. And we know Him because He came to Bethlehem long ago. "It is the unity of present and future in the eternal life, manifested and offered in Jesus Christ, that is the secret of New Testament eschatology."[2]

And so if we put anyone or anything else at the center of interest in our thinking about the *eschaton,* we are sure to fall into error. There is no center, no key, but Christ. The one who came to reveal the Father, who was crucified for us on the cross, who rose triumphant from the dead, who ascended to the right hand of the Father, is the one who must come and who will come. ". . . the end does not come 'of itself'; it is He who brings it. Eschatology is therefore concerned, not so much with the 'last things' as with Him who is 'the first and the last.' This explains why in seeing Him the New Testament witnesses were able to see the coming Kingdom as an already dawning reality, and why

1 A. Roy Eckardt, "Land of Promise and City of God," *Theology Today,* January, 1954.
2 J. E. Fison, *The Christian Hope* (Longmans, 1954), p. 36.

the resurrection of Christ was the mainspring of faith in the Second Coming."[3] In the fullness of times all things, both in heaven and in earth, will be summed up in Him.[4] But we do not hope for Christ's return simply as an event in the future. That return is inseparably bound up with the first appearance of Emmanuel, and with daily fellowship with Him even now. The Morrow belongs to the one who "is already the boundary of our lives."[5]

Therefore the person and work of Christ cannot be seen completely without the Parousia and all the accompaniments and consequences of that Coming. The Christology section of our systematic theologies cannot be separated from the eschatology. The system of God's dealing with the world through Christ must be seen as a grand whole. God has chosen to reveal Himself through His Son. "No man hath seen God at any time; the only begotten Son, who is in the bosom of the Father, he hath declared him."[6] This unveiling first came in the Incarnation. In Christ we beheld His glory. But there will be further unveiling when Christ comes in His own glory. God has much more to show, but the veil of flesh hangs between. When Christ comes again we shall see Him as He is, not in the body of His humiliation, but in His intrinsic glory. Now we can know Him only in part, but then we shall know Him even as He knows us. The final coming of Christ "will be, in His own time, the Final Denouement of God . . . the One who lives in unapproachable Light, the One whom no mortal eye has ever seen or ever can see."[7]

3 W. Schweitzer, *Eschatology and Ethics* (World Council of Churches, Geneva, 1951), p. 7.

4 Eph. 1:10.

5 *Second Report of the Advisory Commission,* World Council of Churches (New York, 1952), p. 7.

6 John 1:18.

7 I Tim. 6:14, 15 (Phillips).

The Parousia will fully reveal the implications of what Christ has already accomplished. Here is a brief summary of that which shall be seen in fullness only when He comes. "When He returns, that will be the resurrection of the dead; but already we live as participants of His risen life. When He returns, that will be the day of inheritance; but already we live as sons of the Father in heaven. When He returns, that will be the final destruction of evil; but already the powers of evil have been dethroned. When He returns, that will be the restoration of creation's lost harmony; but already the powers of the Kingdom are at work to heal and restore. When He returns, that will be the union of the church with her Bridegroom; but already the Lord lives in the midst of His church. When He returns, that will be the final judgment and the consummation of history; but already the judgment of this world has begun."[8]

Here is the tension between the *now* and the *then* concerning which we wrote above. The present work of Christ cannot appear in its true light apart from the larger fulfillment of which it is a prophecy. Take, for instance, His mediatorial work. He came as a priest to make purification for sin.[9] He offered up Himself to make an atonement. On the basis of that sacrifice He has become an intercessor or advocate with the Father in our behalf. He has passed into the heavens where, at the right hand of God, He intercedes for us. But this is something of an interim function. The saving process comes to an end when our salvation is complete. The advocacy can stop when the case is won. "With joy our Saviour will set us in the presence of God's glory."[10] Christ's eternal function is rather that of King than of

8 *Second Report, ut supra,* p. 8.
9 Heb. 1:8.
10 Jude 24.

Priest. He shall reign with those whom He has saved. His coming will bring in that final state of sovereignty.

It is sometimes argued whether we are saved now or whether our salvation is future. In the light of what we have seen of the paradox of the *already* and the *not yet,* it is obvious that salvation is both present and future. "Christ Jesus came into the world to save sinners."[11] And He did save them. Paul's language is, "who saved us."[12] But he also said we are saved by hope, and that "salvation is nearer to us than when we first believed."[13] Peter writes of "a salvation ready to be revealed in the last time."[14] John the Revelator heard a "great voice in heaven, saying, *Now* is come the salvation . . . of his Christ."[15] The New Testament clearly thinks of salvation in eschatological terms. But the eschatological process has already begun. We are saved now, but the full issues of that salvation will be made manifest only when Christ comes back again.

Similarly with regard to the New Testament word redemption, which is synonymous with salvation. Paul says, "we have our redemption through his blood."[16] But only a few lines below he speaks of the day when "we may finally come into full possession of redemption's prize."[17] It is for the day of redemption that we are sealed by the Holy Spirit. It is a wonderful thing to experience now the redemption that is in Christ, to be blessedly redeemed "from the curse of the law."[18] But it is a matter of experience that we wait for the full effect of that redemption. Our bodies are not yet redeemed.[19] There are certain effects of bondage which adhere to this time and place. It is good to

11 I Tim. 1:15.
12 II Tim. 1:9.
13 Rom. 13:11.
14 I Pet. 1:5.
15 Rev. 12:10.

16 Eph. 1:7.
17 Eph. 1:14 (Williams).
18 Gal. 3:13.
19 Rom. 8:23.

be able to look up because our redemption, our full redemption which is yet future, draws near.[20] The consummation of redemption comes at the end. Present redemption is a shadow of that yet to come.

Likewise ". . . with regard to his sanctification the believer in Christ shares in the anticipation of the future. It is the fundamental motif of all New Testament ethics that upon the basis of the Holy Spirit and by faith in the work performed by Christ, man *is* that which he *will become* only in the future, that he is already sinless, already holy, although this becomes full reality only in the future. Thus faith in the Christ-event already permits the disciple of Christ to 'taste the powers of the future world' (Hebrews 6:5)."[21] Christ was the image of God, a perfect reflection of the divine holiness. And God has foreordained that we, His chosen ones, should "be conformed to the image of his Son."[22] By His means of grace He is even now transforming us into that holy likeness "from glory to glory." The change is already great, at which we humbly marvel. We who "once lived in the lusts of our flesh, doing the desires of the flesh and of the mind" are growing "into a holy temple in the Lord."[23] We have already "put on the new man . . . created in righteousness and holiness."[24] But the process of sanctification is not completed. The more holiness we may achieve, the more we see we need. Holy people always feel like praying, "Make me holy." We strive to attain, to be obedient and exemplary disciples. We want to be like Him in complete separation from all sin. We never give up, nor hide behind the excuse of our human weakness. But still we do come short. We know that we shall be like Him

20 Luke 21:28.
21 Oscar Cullmann, *Christ and Time* (Westminster, 1950), p. 75.
22 Rom. 8:29.
23 Eph. 2:3, 22.   24 Eph. 4:24.

only when we shall see Him as He is. It is this hope of perfection when He comes to perfect His work in us which makes us continue in the effort to purify ourselves.[25] Only by His coming may the ideal of holiness be reached. Only in the final glory will we be perfectly conformed to His image.

When Christ was here in His earthly ministry He made claims which seemed preposterous to those who did not believe the claims. He claimed to be the long-looked-for Messiah. But He came in humility, which did not fit the Jewish expectations. Judaism thought of the Messiah as coming in power and glory. "Why didn't He do something?" one Jewish friend said to me when I urged the claims of Christ as the Messiah. It was a good question. The Messiah ought to do what it was prophesied He would do. Now we believe that Jesus did fulfill many Messianic functions when He was here. At Nazareth He said, "Today hath this scripture been fulfilled in your ears."[26] When He died a redemptive, atoning death on the cross He fulfilled the great Servant prophecy of Isaiah 53. But there are some Messianic functions which admittedly He did not carry out. He did not bring the Day of the Lord whose holy wrath so many of the prophets had described. He did not bring in "the day of vengeance of our God."[27] Those who are not ready to admit that the church is a Messianic community ask for the more striking evidences that Christ was the Messiah He claimed to be. The complete demonstration of His Messiahship awaits events which have not yet occurred. *"Wer sagt 'Messias,' sagt auch 'Eschatologie,' "* said Mowinckel.[28]

25 I John 3:2, 3.
26 Luke 4:21.
27 Isa. 61:2.
28 Quoted from Beutzen by John Bright, "Faith and Destiny," *Interpretation,* January, 1951.

It takes a Second Coming to give final verification to the Messianic claim.

He claimed also to be the Son of God. This claim was not only preposterous; it was blasphemous, if it was not really true. For this blasphemy the Sanhedrin condemned Him to death. The unbelief of the Jews is of course a terrible thing. But one can understand how, in the light of their preconceptions, He did not act like the Son of God. The theophanies of Jewish apocalyptic were manifestations of great power and glory. The Jews thought that when God really was revealed to the world, no one would have to make any claims. The Revelation would speak for itself. He would not be like this meek and unresisting prisoner before them. And so, when Caiaphas stormed, "I adjure thee by the living God, that thou tell us whether thou art the Christ, the Son of God," Jesus followed His affirmation with the prophecy, "Henceforth ye shall see the Son of man sitting at the right hand of Power, and coming on the clouds of heaven."[29] That is, what they think they should see in an apocalypse, they will see. When He returns, His sublime claim to deity will have a sublime verification. The culmination of the divine unveiling will supply what seems, to shortsighted and unbelieving men, to be lacking in God's revelation of Himself through the One who claimed to be His Son.

One of the striking incidents related in the Gospels is that of the Transfiguration. On the mountain Jesus privileged three of His disciples to see Him in His essential glory. Nothing came upon Him there which did not belong to the inward glory of His character and His being. But in His ordinary appearance before men His glory was under a veil. Only this once did it clearly shine through. Peter, one of

29 Matt. 26:64.

the three observers, later wrote that on this occasion they
were eyewitnesses of His majesty.[30] It was a majesty stream-
ing from His inward splendor. They saw Him here as He
really was, perfect in His glory. The subject of discussion
on the mountain was the events soon to take place at the
climax of His ministry. But the cross was humiliation, sor-
row, and suffering. Peter saw here what he afterwards
wrote, that the sufferings of Christ should be followed by
His glory.[31] In fact, he said that when they finally told the
story of the Transfiguration they were making known "the
power and coming of our Lord Jesus Christ."[32] When He
comes again, it will be in power and glory. The Transfiguration was a shadow, a preview, of that which is to come. Then
men shall see Him as He is, with all the outburst of heavenly magnificence which is His own. Then He shall no longer
be in the body of His humiliation, but in the white efful-
gence of His glory. Because He was willing to be the Suffering Servant which Isaiah prophesied, because He was willing to descend from the gleaming whiteness of the Holy
Mount to the anguished darkness of Calvary, God has high-
ly exalted Him and restored Him to the unveiled glory
which He had with the Father before the world was. In that
glory we shall see Him at the Parousia. Then every tongue
shall confess the truth of His claims, for there will be left
no excuse or ground of rejection.

"The Transfiguration narrative," writes Robinson, "is not
intended to throw into doubt the divinity of the humiliated
Christ by contrast with an ultimate, exalted state. On the
contrary, it is a turning back of the corner of the veil to reveal the essential, the eschatological, glory which now is,
and which constitutes the real truth about the present hu-

30 II Pet. 1:16.
31 I Pet. 1:11.
32 II Pet. 1:16.

5

miliation." Here is another illustration of the coexistence of that which is passing and that which is coming. "The eclipse of the old order is yet only partial, but the sun has begun to move across its disk. Christians, as those who belong to the new and yet who still inhabit the old, live, as it were, in the area of intersection: they are those upon whom the 'ends of the ages' have overlapped (the probable meaning of *katenteken* in I Corinthians 10:11)."[33]

We have now examined the first reason why an eschatological future is necessary—Christ must come back to complete the work and the witness He began. As Peters put it, "The First Advent brings the saving grace, but the Second perfects it; the First brought the earnest of redemption in humiliation, the Second completes it in glory."[34] And we conclude in the words of Minear: ". . . what really constitutes the object of hope is the completion of Christ's *work* among men. It is not accurate to say that the object of hope is merely the visible return of Christ. *What happens when* He returns is of chief significance. His revelation marks the horizon of a living hope because what is now the assured ground of hope will then be manifested throughout the world. What is now true in the heavenly places will then permeate the whole creation. And this manifestation will include the appearance of a purified community of sons made wholly like Him. Creation will be pervaded and dominated by the fullness of His glory. . . ."[35]

33 J. A. T. Robinson, *In the End God* (Clark, 1952), pp. 60 f.

34 *Theocratic Kingdom* (Kregel, 1952), III, p. 312.

35 Paul S. Minear, *Christian Hope and the Second Coming* (Westminster, 1954), p. 94.

V

THE SPIRITUAL MATURITY
OF THE REDEEMED

A second need for an eschatological denouement is that
the redeemed may be brought into spiritual maturity. The
Christian life and experience always has an eye on the
future. Even at its best it has something of an interim character. There is in the New Testament, not a note of satisfied achievement, but of becoming. As Vos says, ". . . the
entrance upon the Christian state is . . . semi-eschatological
in import; . . . in principle the believer has been translated
into the higher world of the new aeon. . . . [There is] a
vital relationship between what is enjoyed already, and
what will be received at the end, for it is characteristic of
the principle to lead on into the final fulfillment."[1] After
citing Romans 6:5, 11 on the relationship of the resurrection to victorious living, and II Corinthians 3:8 on the
connection between the glory of Christ and our progressive
sanctification, Vos continues: ". . . a transforming influence
proceeds from Christ, such an influence as He could bring
to bear upon us only in the capacity of the glorified, i.e.,
the risen Christ, and which has for its goal the acquisition
of the same glory image on the part of the believers."

Our relation to Christ in faith is very frequently referred
to as eternal life. "He that believeth hath eternal life."[2]

1 Geerhardus Vos, *Pauline Eschatology* (Eerdmans, 1952), p. 157.
2 John 6:47.

"The free gift of God is eternal life."[3] The word "eternal"
immediately gives the life which we have in and through
Christ a character that looks beyond the present age: "The
mere fact of the frequency of the conjunction of 'life' with
'aionios' (about 45 times) shows how eminently eschatological the conception of life grew to be from the simplest
beginnings."[4]

Life is basic. It is being, in contrast to nonbeing. There
is no more fundamental antithesis of the Scriptures than
that of life and death. Life is union with God through
Christ; death is separation from God. Life is a thing so
absolutely precious that there is ecstasy in knowing that
life in Christ exists "unto the Ages."[5] "In Christ" gives it
quality; "eternal" gives it indefinite extension. "The deep-
est mystical verity in soteriology and Christology is found
to join itself to the eschatological prospect."[6]

But we have this life already. "God gave unto us eternal
life."[7] John writes, "that ye may know that ye have [present
tense] eternal life."[8] From the death of our sins Christ has
raised us to life. In him we have been made alive. Living
daily with Christ is a precious reality. Here again, however,
is the now familiar paradox, the tension between that which
is and that which is not yet. This life which we have we
also seek for. "Those who by persistently doing right strive
. . . will have eternal life."[9] "He that soweth unto the Spirit
shall of the Spirit reap eternal life."[10] Life is a promise to
which we look forward. In one passage Paul gets the two

3 Rom. 6:23.
4 Vos, *op. cit.*, p. 303.
5 Weymouth's usual translation of *aionios.*
6. Vos, *op, cit.,* p. 309.
7 I John 5:11.
8 I John 5:13.
9 Rom. 2:7 (Goodspeed).
10 Gal. 6:8.

tenses together: "having promise of the life which now is, and of that which is to come."[11]

Now obviously the life present and the life to come are connected. One is the continuation of the other. The stage of life now in realization is a prophecy and a promise of that which is to come. And the second stage of our life can come only as the Source of that life brings it in. "When Christ, who is our life, shall be manifested, then shall ye also with him be manifested in glory."[12] Only those who have life now will participate in the eternal extension of that life. And if anyone should deny the reality of the life to come, what meaning or value could there be left for the spiritual life which is given us here? There is between the life which we have and the life which shall be given us an unbreakable continuity. "The life hereafter will therefore not be a new life but rather the life which a man 'in Christ' already has, only lived under new and unimaginably glorious conditions. . . . The relationship of 'in Christ' will have given place to that of being 'with Christ,' and our 'lowly bodies' will have become like His 'glorious' body.' "[13]

Christians are also spoken of as heirs. Paul writes to the Romans and to the Galatians that because we are the children of God we are also His heirs. This fact is given an evident eschatological reference in Titus 3:7, "heirs according to the hope of eternal life," in Hebrews 6:17, "heirs of the promise," and in James 2:5, "heirs of the kingdom which he promised." Paul was looking to the future when he told the elders of Ephesus that the Word was able to give them "the inheritance among all them that are sanctified,"[14] and when he wrote to the Colossians,

11 I Tim. 4:8.
12 Col. 3:4.
13 Archibald M. Hunter, "The Hope of Glory," *Interpretation*, April, 1954.
14 Acts 20:32.

"from the Lord ye shall receive the recompense of the inheritance."[15] The many references to inheriting the Kingdom or eternal life are obviously eschatological.

We have no complaint to make of our present possession. The pinnacle of life on earth is our glorious fellowship with Christ. We are not poverty-stricken waifs waiting dismally for our ship to come in. The joy and peace and sense of satisfaction we already have make us rich beyond description. But all this is only a foretaste of the inheritance laid up for us. The New Testament speaks with ecstasy and wonder of that which is yet to be ours. With the gift of Christ God has given us everything else.[16] The present and the future . . . all belongs to us.[17] We have now only the first installment of future bliss,[18] but this is a guarantee that we shall have full possession.[19] Our inheritance is imperishable, unsullied, unfading, and it is being kept safe in heaven for us.[20] The divine covenant is the assurance that promised inheritance shall be ours.[21] We need not be troubled with a sense of unworthiness, for He has qualified us to receive our share of the inheritance.[22]

And all this when He comes to give to us our full heritage!

The same language of a pledge for future fulfillment is used with reference to the Holy Spirit. In three places Paul says the Spirit is given to us as an earnest, a pledge, a down payment which guarantees still greater things to come.[23]

The promise of Jesus when He was here was that He would send the Spirit to dwell in His disciples. He would be power and wisdom to them. That promise was fulfilled

15 Col. 3:24.
16 Rom. 8:32.
17 I Cor. 3:22.
18 II Cor. 5:5.
19 Eph. 1:14.

20 I Pet. 1:4 (Goodspeed).
21 Heb. 9:15.
22 Col. 1:12 (Weymouth).
23 II Cor. 1:22; 5:5; Eph. 1:14.

at Pentecost. It was a momentous occasion when God came and touched human life in a new and dynamic way through His Spirit. It was the beginning of the church. It made the disciples flaming witnesses of the Gospel. Filled with the Spirit, they had insights and courage and abilities which they never had before. Walking in the power of the Spirit, they had strength to resist Satan, his temptations and his obstructions. The Spirit wrought in them the fruit of righteousness and holiness. The life in the Spirit became that new thing which implanted the new aeon in the old, which began now in the realm of the flesh that indwelling which shall be in a more complete fashion the order of the eternal state.

Pentecost was a coming of God to man. Every coming of the Spirit to the Christian has been an effective realization of the presence of God in the earthly and temporal realm. It has been argued by some that Pentecost was the Second Coming of Christ. As an explanation of the eschatology of the New Testament this is ridiculously inadequate. But there is a sense in which Pentecost was the Second Coming. We must remember that "First Coming" and "Second Coming" are not the vocabulary of Scripture. The future Coming is the last of a series of comings. The first coming of God to man was the advent of Emmanuel, incarnated for the purpose of redemption, and to usher in the new age. Shortly after this coming was terminated by the Ascension, God came again as the Holy Spirit fell at Pentecost. He has kept on coming to the spiritual successors of the one hundred and twenty in the upper room. He will come again in the Parousia, when time shall end. The Parousia must be thought of, not as standing alone, but as "the sequel of all previous revelations of Christ to the world."[24]

24 Geo. P. Eckman, *When Christ Comes Again* (Abingdon, 1917).

Our era has been called the dispensation of the Spirit. Certainly the Spirit has great and important functions to perform in the world now. But His primary functions are in the eternal world when spirit rules supreme. Vos says that in Paul's writings "the Spirit is viewed as pertaining specifically to the future life, nay, as constituting the substantial make-up of this life, and the present possession of the Spirit is regarded in the light of an anticipation. The Spirit's proper sphere is the future aeon; from thence He projects Himself into the present, and becomes a prophecy of Himself in His eschatological operations. . . . The eschatological state is pre-eminently a pneumatic spiritual state . . . the highest form of life known."[25]

What the Spirit does now in and for a Christian He will do then, only in a manner infinitely greater. The present life in the Spirit, therefore, should be oriented toward the future. What an incentive for yielded living! The Holy Spirit, already at work in us, is preparing us for that perfectly spiritual life of the eternal state. The present life in the Spirit is only a token, a shadow, of that which shall be when flesh through the resurrection has been made completely amenable to Spirit rule. "The 'groaning' of the Spirit for the consummation . . . expresses . . . the pain at the continued delay of the fulfillment, in which the Spirit will affect even the bodies; and the joyous knowledge of the already decided victory."[26] "The new thing that the 'Victory Day' brings . . . is that the Holy Spirit . . . lays hold of the entire world of flesh. . . . At the end . . . the Spirit, which already dwells in us, will also 'lay hold of our mortal bodies' (Romans 8:11)."[27]

25 *Op. cit., passim*, Ch. VI.
26 Cullmann, *Christ and Time* (Westminster, 1950).
27 *Ibid.*, p. 141.

The Christian, then, living in the light and power of the Holy Spirit, is as yet enjoying only a partial, a provisional dominance by the Spirit. That life is eschatological, prophetic of the ultimate spiritual reality which shall follow the resurrection at the Parousia. Then the life of the Spirit shall lay by its temporal wrappings.

One point yet concerns us. The highest expression of the Christian life is worship. That the creature should adore and honor and praise the Creator is fitting. The child of God loves the hour of private or public worship, where spirit is aware of the promised presence, and pours out the offering of love and adoration. In song or testimony, in sacrament or offering, there is a consciousness of the unseen presence. "Lo, I am with you," promised our Lord. "Maranatha," responds the worshiping community. That phrase, preserved for us in I Corinthians 16:22, may be a prayer for His presence in any gathering of the saints. As such it is a fitting expression for any worshiper. But His spiritual presence with us, real and blessed as it is, speaks to our longing hearts of a Presence which only the Parousia can provide. Then we shall see Him. Then we shall sing our Hallelujahs as we can never sing them here. In fact, some of our present worship forms will lose their meaning altogether. The Lord's Supper we shall eat only "till he come."[28] And so Maranatha is usually interpreted as a prayer for the Lord's Coming. "May the Lord come soon!" Phillips translates it. "Our Lord is coming" is Williams' rendering. "Even so, come," our hearts echo. For we shall worship Him better when His presence teaches us how.

"Glory be to the Father, and to the Son, and to the Holy Ghost, as it was in the beginning, is now, and ever shall be, world without end. Amen."

28 I Cor. 11:26.

Let us close with these words of Vos: "The time when God gathers His fruit is the joyous vintage-feast of all high religion. The value of a work lies in its ultimate product. Consequently, where religion entwines itself around a progressive work of God, such as redemption, its general responsiveness becomes prospective, cumulative, climacteric; it gravitates with all its inherent weight toward the end. A redemptive religion without eschatological interest would be a contradiction in terms."[29]

29 Geerhardus Vos, "Eschatology of the Psalter," *Princeton Theological Review,* January, 1920.

VI

THE PERFECTION
OF THE KINGDOM

In the previous lectures, besides giving a brief history of eschatology and showing that the predictions of the Bible, particularly of the New Testament, are our only source of knowledge concerning the future, we have set forth our main thesis. This is that Christ must be the end as He is the beginning, the Omega as well as the Alpha. When He came in His incarnation He began many things which require completion. The climax of the drama of redemption, which occurred within a few days in the Crucifixion, the Resurrection, and Pentecost, calls for a denouement. That denouement will come when Christ returns. Between the First Coming and the Second Coming we live in a tension between what has already occurred and what is yet to happen. Present spiritual blessings speak on every hand of promised enlargement and fulfillment. New Testament eschatology teaches us to orient our thought and our lives to what God holds in store for us when time shall end, and we shall live with Christ eternally. But the future is a continuation and fuller development of what God has already done for man in the incarnational accomplishment of Christ. The Christian looks two ways, as the communion memorial symbolizes: back to the "finished work" of Christ, forward to that which can be completed only by the Parousia. The New Age which Christ brought in coexists with the

Old Age in which sin and death rule. The denouement will bring the old to an end, and set the new free in its full glory and spiritual character.

We have discussed two reasons why Christ must come again: to complete His work among men, and to bring His people into a full realization of their spiritual potential. We proceed now to a further study of the loose ends which must be gathered in by the Parousia.

Christ must come to perfect His Kingdom. The kingdom concept is one of the most important of the many used to depict the relation between God and His people. Christ came preaching the Gospel of the Kingdom, announcing that it had arrived.[1] The apostles preached the Kingdom of God as they taught concerning the Lord Jesus Christ.[2] Sinners were called to become subjects of the Kingdom.[3] God is praised as the King of the Ages.[4] "The kingdom of God," says Ladd, "is the sovereign rule of God, manifested in the person and work of Christ, creating a people over whom He reigns, and issuing in a realm or realms in which the power of His reign is realized."[5]

The idea of God's right to rule grows, of course, out of the creation. He made men to bring Him praise by doing His will. God's creation must fulfill His plan. When men take their own way, contrary to God's way, the plan is spoiled. Throughout history God woos men, for their happiness and for His glory, to submit to His rule. At the end of history all that opposes His will is destroyed and the purpose of the creation is realized in a Kingdom completely in harmony with His sovereignty.

1 Matt. 9:35 *et al.*
2 Acts 28:31.
3 I Thess. 2:12.
4 Rev. 15:3.
5 George E. Ladd, *Crucial Questions About the Kingdom of God* (Eerdmans, 1952), p. 80.

The kingdom concept has its beginning in the Old Testament. The prophets frequently speak of a coming reign, although the phrase "Kingdom of God" does not occur. "The reign of God is constantly pictured . . . as an era of unparalleled good. . . . That a future Golden Age was in the purpose and promise of God is emphatically declared again and again by the Hebrew prophets."[6] The line of David was to be continued. The Messiah Prince would come to Jerusalem and reign in righteousness and peace. Though the chief emphasis is upon a rule over God's chosen people Israel, it is made plain also that there should be a world-wide Kingdom in which men of all nations might participate. This Kingdom was thought of as coming at the end of history. It would be the vindication of God in His contention with the earth's peoples, and the final assertion of His sovereignty.

This future Kingdom was most clearly pictured by Daniel. A series of great world empires would be destroyed and succeeded by an everlasting Kingdom. The Messianic Kingdom was to be set up in the days of the other kings by the God of heaven, and would fill the whole earth. This Kingdom, said Daniel, will endure forever.

But the prophets introduced another note about the coming Messiah-Prince. Isaiah told that ". . . the victory of that kingdom . . . will be procured not by force or spectacular power, but by the sacrificial labors of God's Servant. Here we learn of man's resistance to the Kingdom, a resistance so bitter that it will cost the blood of the Servant. . . . God proposes to win His Kingdom through the vicarious sacrifice of His Servant."[7] And Daniel foretells that the Anointed One will make reconciliation for iniquity, and

6 Roderic Dunkerley, *The Hope of Jesus* (Longmans, 1953), p. 5.
7 John Bright, *The Kingdom of God* (Abingdon, 1953), pp. 149 f.

will be cut off and have nothing.[8] This was a conception of the Messiah that was obviously difficult to harmonize with that of a mighty conquering king.

The Kingdom, according to the Old Testament, is to come when the King comes. And so the people of Jesus' day were expecting a king who would deliver them from the Roman oppressor and set up a triumphant Kingdom at Jerusalem. Jesus came announcing that the Kingdom was at hand. But He did not act like the king the religious leaders and interpreters were expecting, and they rejected Him. In His life and death Jesus fulfilled the picture of the Suffering Servant and the Saviour from sin. But still He claimed to be the King. "I must preach the good tidings of the kingdom of God . . . for therefore was I sent."[9] "My kingdom is not of this world."[10] When Pilate asked Him whether He was a king, He replied, "Certainly I am a king."[11] So well known was His claim that His executioners put over His head on the cross this superscription, "The King of the Jews." It was a taunting jeer of unbelievers. Did a poor man hanging on a cross look the part of a king?

After His resurrection He kept up the kingly speech. "All authority hath been given unto me in heaven and on earth."[12] That sets the tone for all of the New Testament. "To the Old Testament the fruition and victory of God's Kingdom was always a future, indeed an eschatological, thing, and must always be spoken of in the future tense. . . . But in the New Testament we encounter a change: the tense is a resounding present indicative—the Kingdom is here. . . . The New Testament saw Jesus . . . as the Christ, the prom-

8 Dan 9:24, 26.
9 Luke 4:43.
10 John 18:36.
11 John 18:37 (Williams).
12 Matt. 28:18.

ised Messiah, who was to set up His Kingdom. It hailed Him as the fulfillment of law and prophecy," the realization of the hope of Israel.[13]

Hear the New Testament witness. Peter said to the high priest, "Him did God exalt with his right hand to be a Prince and a Saviour."[14] Paul said that God "translated us into the kingdom of the Son of his love,"[15] and to Timothy he wrote, 'I' . . . implore you, in the presence of . . . Christ Jesus . . . and by His . . . Kingship. . . ."[16] Peter wrote, ". . . thus shall be richly supplied unto you the entrance into the eternal kingdom of our Lord and Saviour Jesus Christ."[17]

The New Testament tells us that the Kingdom is now here. Phillips translates the announcement of Jesus, "The Kingdom of Heaven has arrived." Our Lord asserted as He cast out demons, "then is the kingdom of God come upon you."[18] When the Pharisees asked Jesus when the Kingdom was coming, He replied, in Hebert's paraphrase, "You Pharisees are watching for the Kingdom of God, and you are sure that you will be the first to greet it when it comes, and say, 'Lo, here.' But you are wrong: not in looking for it, but in the assumption that when it comes you will be able to recognize it. And it has come and it is here in your midst and you have not had eyes to see."[19] Peter in his Pentecost sermon said that by the resurrection Jesus had been set on David's throne.[20] The early Christians had a lively sense of belonging to Christ's Kingdom now. "Two

13 John Bright, *op. cit.*, pp. 197 f.
14 Acts 5:31.
15 Col. 1:13.
16 II Tim. 4:1 (Weymouth).
17 II Pet. 1:11.
18 Luke 11:20.
19 Luke 17:20, 21, paraphrase by A. G. Hebert, in *The Throne of David* (Faber and Faber, London, 1941), p. 156.
20 Acts 2:30, 31.

words," says Hunter, "summed up the earliest Christian confession of faith—*Kurios Jesus*, 'Jesus is Lord'; and when the first Christians uttered them they were not merely conferring on Jesus an honorific title; they were affirming, with the full force of their hearts and minds, that Jesus was *now ruling* over God's people and God's world."[21]

On the Kingdom's being now present, Salmond says, "The Kingdom is a present thing, and that in a twofold sense. It is present, in so far as Christ brings it with Him, and embodies it in Himself, and it is present in so far as it has a true, though partial, realization in those who attach themselves to Him, and in their lives give instance of the righteousness which makes the Kingdom. The first gains of the kingly rule, the beginning of the society, are seen in them."[22] George Fox said to the Fifth Monarchy Men of England, who were trying to bring in the Divine Reign by political means, "Christ is already come and doth dwell in the hearts of His people."[23]

There have been three interpretations concerning the time of the Kingdom. One is that the Kingdom is entirely future, and that Jesus merely announced that it was coming. This view has been held, strange to say, by two very different schools of thought. One is the dispensationalists, who say that there can be no kingdom when the king is absent. The Kingdom was postponed, they say, when the Jews rejected it, and will come only when Christ comes back to set up His throne in the millennial reign. The other school is the thoroughgoing eschatologists, represented

20 Acts 2:30, 31.
21 Archibald M. Hunter, "The Hope of Glory," *Interpretation*, April, 1954.
22 S. D. F. Salmond, *Christian Doctrine of Immortality* (T. & T. Clark, Edinburgh, 1895, p. 296.
23 Quoted by Douglas V. Steere, "Hope of Glory and This Present Life," *Theology Today*, October, 1953.

by Albert Schweitzer, who hold that Jesus mistakenly thought He would be returning very soon to establish His reign. These two groups agree on this much, that there is no Kingdom of Christ in the world now.

The second interpretation is that the Kingdom is present, and only present. That is, it belongs to this age, and is to be brought in gradually by the efforts of good men, who invite others to join the Kingdom and help to realize it. This view was very popular a half a century ago, but, as we have seen, is being increasingly abandoned by its disillusioned exponents. It was based on an optimistic human philosophy of progress rather than upon a study of what the Bible says.

The third view is that the Kingdom is already present, but only in a limited, partial form. In Christ the Kingdom of God has come, but it has not yet fully come. It has broken in upon and is operating in this present world, but its ultimate realization is still awaited as a future act of God.[24]

The New Testament, while it teaches that the Kingdom is present, also teaches that it is future. Jesus speaks of the time when He will drink with His disciples in the Father's Kingdom.[25] Because His hearers "supposed that the kingdom of God was immediately to appear," He told them a parable of a nobleman who was going to a "far country, to receive for himself a kingdom, and to return."[26] To His disciples He said, "I appoint unto you a kingdom," in a setting which makes it clearly eschatological. Paul says that if we endure, we shall also reign with Christ.[27] He is confident that the Lord will deliver him, and save him "unto

24 W. Schweitzer, *Eschatology and Ethics* (World Council of Churches, Geneva, 1951), p. 5.
25 Matt. 26:29.
26 Luke 19:11, 12.
27 II Tim. 2:12.

his heavenly kingdom."[28] At the sounding of the seventh
angel John the Revelator heard heavenly voices saying,
"The kingdom of the world is become the kingdom of our
Lord, and of his Christ: and he shall reign for ever and
ever."[29]

It seems clear, then, that the Scriptures teach that the
Kingdom comes with Christ. It came when He first came.
It is realized now in the hearts and lives of those who are
His. Through their testimony and influence it has its effect
for good in this world. But for its full realization Christ
must come again to bring in the promised Kingdom. Here
again we find the tension between that which is and that
which is not yet, that which has already come and that
which is yet to come. Those who acknowledge Christ as
their Lord and King find in the present stage of the Kingdom great joy and sense of fulfillment. But they see many
things "not yet . . . subjected to him."[30] They see Satan
still in opposition. They see a world in rebellion. They
know that there are still undefeated enemies. They long
to see their Lord in complete control. They want Him to
assert His sovereignty. And so they look forward with desire for the eschatological Kingdom, when the Kingdom
of God shall be universal and complete.

Students of eschatology have described the two stages of
the Kingdom as follows. Vos: ". . . while the Kingdom is
now actually coming, a complete separation between the
evil and the good cannot be effected until the end of the
world. During the present age the Kingdom must partake
of the limitations and imperfections to which a sinful environment exposes it."[31] von Thadden: "We are not in an

28 II Tim. 4:18.
29 Rev. 11:15.
30 Heb. 2:8.
31 Geerhardus Vos, *The Kingdom and the Church* (Eerdmans, 1951), p. 89.

eschatological waiting room. Jesus is coming again, not to inaugurate the Kingdom, but to complete it."[32] Temple: "There remains a final consummation which involves a change in our mortal state and a removal of our present limitations. The Kingdom cannot come in all its perfection in this world."[33] Bruce: ". . . Jesus did not expect the Kingdom of God during the period of its earthly development to be other than an imperfect, disappointing thing. . . . He believed that the ideal would eventually be realized, that the Kingdom would at length come in all its perfection and purity."[34] Advisory Commission, World Council of Churches: ". . . to affirm His Lordship is also to affirm that the Lordship will be finally manifest."[35] Salmond: "In its present form it has but a partial and relative realization, which looks to a consummation. Now it is in the process of enlargement; hereafter it will come to its goal."[36]

We continue in order to show how widely accepted is this two-stage concept of the Kingdom. Berkhof: "Though the Lord refers to the Kingdom as a present reality, He more often speaks of it as the future state of consummate happiness, in which the whole life of man and of society will be in perfect harmony with the will of God. . . . Clearly the Kingdom of God is ultimately an eschatological concept."[37] Bright: ". . . the Kingdom of God in the New Testament must be understood in a twofold aspect: it has come and is even now in the world; it is also yet to come. In the

32 Reinhold von Thadden, unpublished address at Chicago Temple, August, 1954.

33 William Temple, quoted by T. F. Glasson, *His Appearing and His Kingdom* (Epworth Press, London, 1953), p. 33.

34 A. B. Bruce, *The Kingdom of God* (Clark, 1904), p. 311.

35 *Second Report*, Advisory Commission World Council of Churches (New York, 1952), p. 7.

36 S. D. F. Salmond, *op. cit.*

37 L. Berkhof, *The Kingdom of God* (Eerdmans, 1951), p. 18.

tension between the two the chuch must live, and must always live, as the 'eschatological community.' "[38]

It is important to note that on this point there is agreement between non-millennialists and nondispensational premillennialists. Even a dispensationalist like Geo. H. N. Peters admitted many years ago "that able premillenarians hold to the idea that the church is a provisional or introductory Kingdom."[39] I quote three modern premillennialists. Robert D. Culver: "The fact that believers in the present age are 'translated into the Kingdom' (Col. 1:13), that born-again believers appear to have entered the Kingdom of God (John 3:1 ff.), that the course of the present age is traced as the history of 'the kingdom of heaven' (parables of Matt. 13), and that Kingdom aspects seem to be attached even to the ministry of the Gospel during the church age (cf. Acts 8:12; 15:13-18; 28:23) forbids that we declare every aspect of the Kingdom future."[40] George E. Ladd: "The Kingdom as the reign of God fully realized in all human relations is future; but the Kingdom as the reign of God to be realized in personal experience has come to men now in the person and mission of Christ. So the Kingdom is yet to come, but its powers have already come."[41] J. L. Stauffer: "Premillennialists believe that the *spiritual phase* of the Kingdom of God as preached by John the Baptist and Jesus is now a present reality throughout this age. They do not believe, however, that this spiritual phase fulfills all that is predicted of the Kingdom of God. The future phase begins with the Second Coming of Christ."[42]

38 John Bright, *op. cit.,* p. 237.

39 *Theocratic Kingdom* (Kregel, 1952), I, p. 651.

41 *Op. cit.,* p. 125.

40 Robert D. Culver, *Daniel and the Latter Days* (Revell, 1954).

42 "The Reality and Nature of the Coming Messianic Kingdom," *The Christian Ministry,* January-March, 1955.

We may conclude, then, that most of those who take Bible prophecy seriously are looking forward to the kind of a Kingdom which has only in part been realized. We are striving to live now according to the revealed principles of the Kingdom. Christ our King, as we abide in Him and yield ourselves to a wholehearted discipleship, does make us in fact true subjects of His Realm. We are duty-bound also to do all we can to make His Kingdom manifest in our homes, our churches, our communities, our nation, and our world. We enjoy many blessings in our society—freedom, respect for personality and the rights of others, compassionate care for the unfortunate, confidence and trust in human relations—which are the direct or indirect result of the influence of men and women who belong to Christ's Kingdom. But, as Paul Peachey has written, ". . . the Gospel nowhere visualizes a permanent peace between 'church' and 'world,' nowhere predicts the final harmonization of all that is incongruous in human experience except eschatologically, and nowhere promises the redemption of this aeon *in toto*."[43] Christ's Lordship has been proclaimed, and of His ultimate victory there is no doubt. But as the inauguration of the Kingdom awaited His first coming to the world, so the consummation of that Kingdom awaits His second advent. The present world order, so chronically and persistently resisting the will of God and hostile to His righteousness, must be displaced, through a mighty act of God, by a different order, in which God is recognized, obeyed, and worshiped. This new order, now partly hidden and partly in evidence, shall be fully manifest when our blessed Lord comes to reign in glory.

Is the millennium this final, eternal Kingdom? Obviously

[43] "Toward an Understanding of the Decline of the West," *Concern*, June, 1954.

a reign of only one thousand years is not an eternal Kingdom. A reign upon this earth is not the fully realized heavenly Kingdom. A reign which ends in a massive rebellion is not the Kingdom from which all sin has been completely and finally eliminated.

Our main thesis does not call for a discussion of the millennium. Suffice it here to say that in Revelation 20 we are told by the revelator of a thousand-year reign of Christ and the risen martyrs. The most natural interpretation of this passage is that this reign occurs after Christ returns and before the final resurrection and judgment. It may be assumed that the reign is on this earth, although the passage does not say so.

The Gospels and the Epistles say nothing directly about such a millennial reign. Girdlestone says, ". . . if we had not the twentieth chapter of Revelation, we should know nothing of the Millennium."[44] And no New Testament text says that there will be such a reign over a restored Jewish nation in Jerusalem. Fitting Old Testament Messianic Scriptures into the thousand-year reign of Revelation 20 is reading things into the Bible rather than getting truth out of the Bible by careful exegesis. The reign which the early chiliasts looked for was associated with the return of Christ to carry the Gospel to its triumphant issue. Charles Erdman, a mild premillennialist, has said, "Here is a millennium, and it does follow the return of Christ, but is it of such a character as to contain all the elements and to realize all the features sketched by the rather exuberant fancies of some popular teachers of the Premillennial school? . . . (They) crowd into the rather dim and shadowy limits of this 'Millennium' the fulfillment of predictions that have a wider

---

44 R. H. Girdlestone, *Grammer of Prophecy* (Eyer and Spottiswoode, London, 1901), p. 143.

horizon and belong to ages whose bounds and confines are never named."[45]

Here is one of the areas of prophecy where very little is revealed. Speculation is unwarranted and is dangerous, for soon people will accept our surmises as the clear teaching of the Word. Historical millennialists, who did not go down the dispensational road, were modest and honest in their teaching. Nathaniel West introduced several letters into the 1886 Prophecy Conference from some of the great premillennial commentators. "He received these letters," says C. Norman Kraus, "in answer to questions he had sent to them. Delitzsch says that he is in general agreement but 'I believe in the literal reality of this apocalyptic picture without pressing slavishly the letter.' He comes out clearly against the Jewish national restoration, to which West adds . . . , 'with the protest of Dr. Delitzsch against a reproduction of the Jewish Old Testament earthly and national theocracy, we all most cordially sympathize.' "[46]

Historical premillennialism, without the additions given to it by Darby and his successors, has some real values. Fison approves ". . . a two-stage eschatology in which the purpose of God is achieved by means of a preliminary kingdom of Christ, which is the prelude to the ultimate Kingdom of God. . . . As the sequel . . . to the Parousia, it can be integrated into a coherent Christian eschatology, and is a valuable corrective to merely individualistic and otherworldly interpretations of the Christian hope."[47] The harm comes when interpreters fit details into the picture of the millennium which make it a denial of all the principles of the Kingdom that are taught us in the New Testa-

45 Charles Erdman, *The Return of Christ* (Doran, 1922), pp. 68 ff.
46 C. Norman Kraus, *Dispensationalism—Rise and Development* (unpublished thesis, 1954), p. 73.
47 J. E. Fison, *The Christian Hope* (Longmans, 1954), p. 148.

ment. If there is to be a millennium, we may be sure it will
not be a reversal of the methods of grace and inner renewal.
It is descriptions like the following by George F. Trench
which make the millennium seem anything but a proper
sequel to the Kingdom we know now:

"The nations will be Christ's possessions and the utter-
most part of the earth His inheritance, not by conversion,
but by coercion, to be 'broken in pieces like a potter's ves-
sel,' at their first resistance; held down as the 'footstool at
his feet' throughout that age; and at its end, when in irre-
pressible and incorrigible hostility they dare once more to
lift the rebel hand against Him, to be utterly and finally
destroyed by fire from heaven."[48] Such a regime could hardly by any stretch of Christian imagination be called a Reign
of Peace; in fact, it is no reign at all.

It is important that any millennialism we may hold
should not contradict any principles of salvation or ethics
clearly set forth by Christ and the apostles. But it does not
seem to be too crucial a matter whether we believe in a
thousand-year reign of Christ on the earth after His Return,
or whether we interpret Revelation 20 in some other way.
For few millennialists believe that the millennium is the
final, eternal Kingdom of God. Let us hear what some
of them say.

Charles Erdman: "It may be unreasonable to expect that
all men will agree upon the exact character of the predicted
millennium . . . ; but a millennium is not the goal of
prophecy; this goal is the perfected Kingdom of God upon
earth. . . ."[49]

---

48 Quoted by W. M. Smith, *World Crises and the Prophetic Scriptures*
(Moody, 1953), pp. 331 f.
49 *Op. cit.*, p. 93.

Robert D. Culver: ". . . the millennium is only an initial stage of an everlasting Kingdom."[50]

George E. Ladd: the millennium is a stage "by which this age is to pass away and the age to come be inaugurated, viz., by the agency of an interregnum of Christ on the earth."[51]

Erich Sauer: ". . . the Millennium is still but a portico to eternity. It is the first, lesser, and likewise the introductory period of the coming Kingdom of God. . . . The true essential core of the Perfecting is not the earthly Kingdom of God on the old earth . . . but the eternal, of which that will be only the court and porch of the second and chief portion of the coming Kingdom of God, even the nations on the new earth with the new Jerusalem there."[52]

So there we are! The millennium is not the goal, just a step toward the goal. It is not the everlasting Kingdom, but only an initial stage. It is not the Reign of Christ, but an interregnum. It is not the house in which we live, but only the porch over which we shall walk. And yet one of the chief points at issue in many discussions of eschatology is whether the house has a porch or not. If the Lord has put a porch on His eternal mansions, we'll walk over it, of course. If He hasn't, then we'll step directly from the street into our Father's House. Perhaps we should be ashamed of the differences which have divided us into schools. Let us get interested in the house, or rather in the Lord of the house. The Kingdom is the thing, not the stages by which we may reach it. We work and pray for the coming of that Kingdom, and anticipate with joy the time

50 *Op. cit.*, p. 124.
51 *Op. cit.*, p. 169.
52 Erich Sauer, *From Eternity to Eternity* (Eerdmans, 1954), p. 169.

when the righteous shall "shine forth as the sun in the Kingdom of their Father."[53]

What is the relation of the Jewish people to the Kingdom teachings of the Bible? Old Testament references to the Messianic Kingdom concerned the Jewish nation chiefly, but not solely. The Jewish nation was to be, not the end, but the means, of world-wide blessing. God chose the Jews because He had chosen to save all mankind. Israel became the channel of revelation by which God could bring salvation to all nations. "They were living predictions, in their relations to God, of the glorious destiny of all mankind in its progressive union with God."[54] Through the Jews came the holy law, the prophetic interpretations, and the rich devotional literature of the Old Testament. From the line of David came Jesus Christ, the revelation of the true God, the agent of eternal salvation, and the Prince of the everlasting Kingdom. Most of the New Testament writers were Jewish believers in Christ. Our debt to the Jews is incalculable. "Salvation is from the Jews."[55]

Shall we therefore promise them a future Jewish Kingdom? But the Kingdom described in the New Testament is not limited to any particular race or people. There is nothing said about the establishment of a kingdom at Jerusalem. The true Jew, says Paul, is a Jew inwardly.[56] The Jerusalem to which all God's people belong is from above.[57] The new Jerusalem is the bride of Christ.[58] Jesus told the woman of Samaria that a believing heart, and not Jerusalem, was the center of worship in the new age. He foretold

53 Matt. 13:43.
54 A. B. Davidson, *Old Testament Prophecy* (Clark, 1912), p. 5.
55 John 4:22.
56 Rom. 2:29.
57 Gal. 4:26.
58 Rev. 21:10.

the destruction of the temple and the city of Jerusalem, the fulfillment of which prophecy in A.D. 70 was, according to a contemporary Jewish theologian, "the great turning point in Jewish history, the first real breach of the historical tradition."[59] In this and the succeeding tragedies of the centuries (in the days of World War II the Jewish population of the world was reduced by one third) there is illustration of the wrath which came upon a people who not only rejected their Messiah, but did their worst to keep Him from being preached to the Gentiles.[60]

What the Christian Church needs to repent of is that she has often had a part in the anti-Semitism which has made the Jews a wandering people. The result has been a deep prejudice against Christ which otherwise might not exist. "If the Jews in the last hundred years have gone the way of political self-redemption, we must see in this first of all the consequences of grave guilt on the part of the church," says K. H. Rengstorf, Chairman of the German Evangelical Committee for Service to Israel. ". . . it has not placed itself in a genuine solidarity of suffering and 'Galuth' (dispersion) with Israel, following its crucified and risen Lord."[61]

The second failure of the church toward Israel is in evangelization. In Romans 9-11, the most significant passage in the New Testament on Jewish-Gentile relations, Paul expresses his deep concern for the salvation of his people, God's chosen, Israel. He insists that God has not cast off His people. There is open to them the same way of faith which has been opened to all men. And a remnant have

---

59 H. J. Shoeps, in *The Church and the Jewish People* (Edinburgh House Press, 1954), p. 64.

60 I Thess. 2:16.

61 In *The Church and the Jewish People, ut supra,* p. 40.

believed. The rest, hardened in unbelief, have been cut off. But there will be a grafting in again when those who were unbelieving shall again be joined to the stock of faith. Their full inclusion (11:12, RSV) in the family of faith will be like a resurrection from the dead. "And thus all Israel shall be saved."[62] The hope that Paul speaks of is a uniting of Jew and Gentile, by faith in Christ, into a common body. He says nothing about a restored Jewish theocracy.

There is an increasing conviction in Christendom that the church is called to bring the Gospel of Christ to the Jewish people, and a faith that the end-time will see a mighty turning to Christ of His brethren according to the flesh. When the World Council at Evanston refused to declare itself on the Jewish question, a statement signed by twenty-four persons from eleven different countries was read before the Assembly. This statement said:

"The New Testament . . . speaks . . . of the 'Fullness' of Israel, when God will manifest His glory by bringing back His 'eldest son' into the one fold of His grace. This belief is an indispensable element of our one united hope for Jew and Gentile in Jesus Christ. Our hope in Christ's coming victory includes our hope for Israel in Christ. . . . To expect Jesus Christ means to hope for the conversion of the Jewish people, and to love Him means to love the people of God's promise.

"In view of the grievous guilt of Christian people toward the Jews throughout the history of the church, we are certain that 'the church cannot rest until the title of Christ to the Kingdom is recognized by His own people according to the flesh.' "[63]

---

62 Rom. 11:26 (Berkeley).
63 Mimeographed copy released at Evanston.

What does the present political State of Israel have to do with the Kingdom of God? The New Testament describes the utter destruction of Jewish national life in a tragedy so eschatological in its significance that the description is coalesced with that of the Second Coming.[64] But nothing is said about its restoration. Old Testament prophecies of a restored nation in the Land make the Messiah the agent of that restoration. "Zionism," says Wilbur M. Smith, "sprang from a soil definitely irreligious, distinctly non-Biblical, and . . . godless."[65] Because of this, because Israel is not a Messianic state, "Extreme [Jewish] orthodoxy cannot and, therefore, does not recognize the present state of Israel."[66] Clearly it is going beyond Scripture to say that present developments in Palestine are a fulfillment of prophecy. As a part of the marvelous story of the preservation of the Jews through the centuries, a unique phenomenon which needs some explanation, events in Palestine are of great interest to believers. But, says Rengstorf, "the church is engaged in a very dangerous venture if it makes any attempt to interpret what is happening in Israel. . . . As a result of events in Palestine it has one more opportunity to show and prove that it is not only a believing church but also a waiting church."[67] We do well to give our chief interest to bringing the Jews to Christ, and leave to God the method and the purpose of the miracle of Jewish preservation.

We have given this much time to the Kingdom because of the large place it holds in the language of the Bible, and because it involves several controversial points. The main point we have made, in connection with our thesis, is that

64 Matt. 24.
65 *Op. cit.,* p. 192.
66 Hans Kosmala, in *The Church and the Jewish People, ut supra,* p. 96.
67 *Op. cit.,* pp. 36 f.

the consummation of the Kingdom of God requires the Second Advent of Christ. We listen to Girdlestone for a résumé on this point: "On turning to the New Testament we are confronted with the appearance of this Kingdom as 'at hand,' and yet when Paul's Epistles were written, and when the Book of Revelation was written, it was in prospect at some time not clearly revealed. The King had come, and seeds of the Kingdom had been sown, subjects were being accumulated; but the coming of the Son of Man in His Kingdom, so graphically described in Matthew, was still in the future. Even when we strip the passages concerning the Kingdom of all that is earthly, national, and political, it is clear that we must look ahead for the fulfillment of the promise."[68]

68 *Op. cit.*, p. 64.

VII

THE DEFEAT OF DEATH

A fourth reason why hope is dependent on the return of Christ is that only so may death be defeated. When sin entered into the world, death came too. "Thou shalt surely die," was the warning of God to the two in Eden, and when they had sinned He gave the formula and pattern of death: "Dust thou art, and unto dust shalt thou return."[1] Ever since, death has been one of the effects of sin in the human race. "Death . . . is the reaction of the divine anger to human rebellion."[2] Death, which is working in us long before our obituaries are written, is the symbol and sign of the destructive character of the sin which is inherent in our sinful nature. But we may be saved from our sin, and that salvation involves also the breaking of the power of death in us.

In the great climactic moment of the drama of redemption Jesus rose from the dead. That is a historic fact which is all-important for us. When our Lord rose from the tomb He broke the strangle hold which death had over the human race. "Christ being raised from the dead dieth no more; death no more hath dominion over him."[3] In His incarnate body He met death, and defeated it. This He could do because He had met sin in His human experience. His death on the cross and His resurrection from the grave

1 Gen. 2:17; 3:19.
2 Emil Brunner, *Eternal Hope* (Westminster, 1954), p. 103.
3 Rom. 6:9.

delivered those who believe in Him from sin and its effects, chief of which is death. There will never need to be a greater demonstration that God is able to conquer all His enemies. Here in the historical fact of the resurrection of Christ we have an objective basis for our faith that the reign and power, both of sin and death, are broken. The apostles preached a risen Lord. They knew the strategic importance of Easter truth. The Resurrection was the leading detail of their *kerygma,* the message they preached, because in that mighty act of God the power of the enemy was broken forever. The confidence they breathed was a new thing in the world. For now it had been demonstrated that evil and death were only temporary, that God had set their limits.

It must be emphasized that the New Testament doctrine of Resurrection is based on the person and the historic action of Christ. Old Testament teaching on the Resurrection was not very clear. Sheol was the land of death. There were only occasional hints of a resurrection from that dread place. The knowledge that God is living led some of His people to faith in a resurrection of the body. But the lines of that doctrine are dimly sketched, and the Sadducees did not believe in it at all. The apostles did not get their vibrant faith in a resurrection from the Jewish background. They believed what they saw with their own eyes after Jesus rose from the dead. Their resurrection faith was not theoretical, but personal. The evidence of the open tomb and the risen Lord convinced them of resurrection truth.

Death was defeated when Jesus rose from the dead. That is, it was defeated in Him, but not in us. There is an interim between the deathblow and the full realization of its effects. We know that because Jesus rose, death must die. But the time for that ultimate victory has not yet come.

Paul wrote, "The last enemy that shall be abolished is death."[4]

Here again is the tension in which we live. Sentence has been pronounced against our archenemy death, but execution day has not come. The final issue is not in doubt, but it is still future. We already live in the power of a Life which is the absolute negation of death. We have been raised with Christ already so far as spiritual privilege and newness of life is concerned. We have eternal life, a life that shall never be hidden under the eclipse of death. We have the sure promise of our Lord, "If a man keep my word, he shall never see death."[5] And yet we hold this treasure of life in bodies which are hastening toward the grave. John died and Paul died and saints of all the centuries died. There is none for whom eventually the bell has not tolled. Unless the Lord comes to stop this funeral procession, we shall all die down in dust. The new life which Christ brought exists in a realm of death. Christ's triumph will not be complete until death is slain.

One of the clearest teachings in the New Testament is that of the resurrection of the body. Jesus said, "For the hour cometh, in which all that are in the tombs shall hear his voice, and shall come forth; they that have done good, unto the resurrection of life; and they that have done evil, unto the resurrection of judgment."[6] After Pentecost the apostles "proclaimed in Jesus the resurrection from the dead."[7] Paul argued before Felix "a resurrection both of the just and unjust,"[8] and in his Epistles a whole theology of resurrection is set forth. Salmond says, "Paul's whole teach-

4 I Cor. 15:26.
5 John 8:51.
6 John 5:28, 29.
7 Acts 4:2.
8 Acts 24:15.

ing . . . on the subject of the future life centers in his doctrine of the Resurrection. Nowhere is that doctrine so magnified; nowhere is it presented with such definiteness. . . . It is in Paul's Epistles above all others that it is set forth as the specifically Christian doctrine."[9] In his Epistles Paul writes chiefly about the resurrection of saints, probably because he was writing to Christian people, but his message to Felix shows that he believed the words of Christ, that all who are in their graves shall come forth. The Revelator calls Christ the "firstborn of the dead,"[10] inferring that others will follow Him in His resurrection.

And the Resurrection will come when Christ comes. Here there is no uncertainty. The Resurrection and the Judgment are associated with the Parousia in language that permits no denial. If we are seeking for a simple, minimal eschatology, here we have it: Jesus is coming again. When He comes there will be a resurrection, a judgment, and an eternal Kingdom. Paul wrote the Thessalonians that when the Lord descends at the trump of God, "the dead in Christ shall rise." He also wrote them that the revelation of the Lord Jesus would bring "eternal destruction" to them "that know not God."[11] Here is an eschatology which we can all believe and teach.

When Paul was at Athens, he preached to the intellectuals there about the Resurrection of Jesus. Some of them mocked at any notion of a bodily resurrection. Why? We know that the Greek philosophers believed in immortality. Plato is famous for his philosophy of life beyond death. Why, then, should the Athenians have mocked?

9 S. D. F. Salmond, *Christian Doctrine of Immorality* (T. & T. Clark, 1895), p. 546.

10 1:5.

11 I Thess. 4:16; II Thess. 1:7-9.

Because they believed in immortality, but not in a resurrection of the body. There is nothing uniquely Christian about a belief in immortality. The Egyptians believed in a life after death. Hinduism believes in the transmigration of souls. And the Greeks developed a dualism which greatly influenced later Christian thought. They taught that the body is evil and mortal. The soul, the noble part of man, is immortal. Death sets the soul free from the evil encumbrance of the body. It is a happy riddance, according to Greek thought.

Many Christian people are more interested in immortality than in resurrection. They have not read the New Testament carefully enough to see that "the Christian faith knows nothing about an immortality of the person. . . ."[12] Such people are only interested in what happens to them and to their loved ones after death. They are curious about what happens on the other side, instead of in the real *Eschaton* of the Scriptures, Christ's final triumph which will raise our bodies and make them like His own glorious body.

Kantonen says: ". . . the question of life after death has been the question of demonstrating the immortality, the death-defying capacity, of the soul. The body is of little consequence. . . . The Christian creed says, not 'I believe in the immortality of the soul,' but 'I believe in the resurrection of the body.' The body is not the antithesis of the soul. . . . It is hard to conceive of a more thorough contrast than the one between Plato and Paul at this point. The New Testament recognizes the body and the soul as two different but not antithetical aspects of human existence. . . . The soul is not a separate part of man, constituting a substance of its own. . . . Man is an indivisible

12 T. A. Kantonen, *The Christian Hope* (Muhlenburg, 1954), p. 33.

whole."[13] And D. T. Niles agrees: "Man is not an immortal soul in a mortal body. Man is body and soul—a total person—in an immortal relationship to God."[14]

Death, then, breaks a unity and totality which must be restored and perfected by a resurrection of the body. The Christian doesn't want to get rid of his body as something evil. He wants to have it redeemed and glorified by the same power which produced the post-resurrection body of Christ. Like Paul, he wants the power of the resurrection now working in him through Christ's Spirit to go on and complete the process to ultimate and final salvation—body and soul, the complete man in the image of Christ.

Such a concept was utterly foreign to the philosophers at Athens. And so they sneered. Likewise there are modern philosophers, some of them who call themselves Christian, who are Greek rather than Christian in their thinking. To them the Resurrection is only a form of speech for immortality. So death brings them the only resurrection they want, and they have no need for a future resurrection at the Parousia. But those who hold New Testament ideas about the body need a Coming to call the dead from their graves.

Where is the soul between death and the Resurrection? Here there is very little revealed. In II Corinthians 5 Paul speaks of a condition of nakedness, without any body, as something from which he shrinks. He longs to be clothed with that heavenly body (Williams) which will finally be his, and of which the Spirit is a first installment. But we are told that for the Christian the intermediate state is one of conscious blessedness in Paradise,[15] in the presence

13 *Ibid.,* pp. 28 ff.
14 D. T. Niles, *Preaching the Gospel of the Resurrection* (Westminster, 1954), p. 66.
15 Luke 23:43.

of Christ. The dying Stephen knew that the Lord Jesus would receive his spirit. And Paul longed to depart and be with Christ, which he knew would be better than life in this sinful world.[16] And yet on this side of the Parousia even the blessed dead have something to desire—being united to their resurrected and changed bodies. Until then their redemption is incomplete; they still belong to the present stage. Says Cullmann, "For the New Testament resurrection faith it is sufficient to have concerning this intermediate state of the dead the one certainty on which alone everything depends, that he who believes in Christ, who is the Resurrection, 'will live, even though he dies' (John 11:25)."[17]

How are the dead raised? It will be a miracle, of course, and we can leave its working to a God who is able to do what He purposes to do. The incredulous must remember the resurrection of our Lord. It is a matter of history that a dead body within a sealed tomb was freed from its wrappings to appear and reappear in a new life at different places and before many witnesses. The resurrection of Christ is both the power and the pattern of that which shall be ours. His resurrection body had certain connections with His pre-resurrection body, such as the wounds, yet it had the power of appearing suddenly behind locked doors. The only certain word we have concerning the nature of the Resurrection is that which Paul gave to the Corinthians—to Greeks who had to have some questions answered.

To them he wrote that it was a body which was raised, but a body which had been changed to fit its post-resurrection condition. It is related to the former body, and yet

16 Phil. 1:23.
17 Oscar Cullmann, *Christ and Time* (Westminster, 1950), p. 241

different from it and superior to it, just as the plant is related to and yet different from the seed from which it sprang. The mortal body and the immortal body, the physical body and the spiritual body, have an "organic continuum."[18] Yet nothing will be found in the new which would be a hindrance to its functions, which are spiritual, and not sensuous.

John Bunyan quaintly described the resurrection change: "The body ariseth, as to the nature of it, the selfsame nature; but as to the manner of it, how far transcendent is it! There is a poor, dry, wrinkled kernel cast into the ground, and there it lieth, and swelleth, breaketh, and, one would think, perisheth; but behold, it receiveth life, it chitteth (i.e., sprouts), it putteth forth a blade, and groweth into a stalk, there also appeareth an ear; it also sweetly blossoms, with a full kernel in the ear: it is the same wheat, yet behold how the form and fashion of that which now ariseth, doth differ from that which then was sown; its glory also when 'twas sown, is no glory, when compared with that in which it riseth. And yet it is the same that riseth that was sown, and no other; though the same after a more glorious manner; not the same with its husk, but without it. Our *bran* shall be left behind us when we rise again."[19]

It is, then, the resurrection of Christ which gives us hope in a world of death. "We are living in a world in which, for all its sin and sadness, Christ has left one vacant tomb in the wide graveyard of the earth, and . . . His victory is like the breach in a North Sea dyke, an event of apparently small importance whose consequences are incalculable. As Heim has stated it, 'Beyond the dyke is the tumultuous

18 J. S. Whale, "Resurrection of the Body and Life Everlasting," *Scottish Journal of Theology*, June, 1949.

19 John Bunyan, *Of the Resurrection of the Dead*, quoted by T. F. Glasson, *His Appearing and His Kingdom* (Epworth, 1953), p. 107.

sea, which will burst through the opening—so Paul knew, when he had met the Risen One, that He is the first-born of them that slept.' "[20]

Our resurrection, the result of His own, will mean the redemption of a whole man, who shall thus find the integrity of his being. It will mean redemptive consummation. It will mean "the largest conceivable perspective into a life of new structure and new potencies for the entire state of the Christian man."[21] It will mean personal separateness and recognition. It will be the death of death, as John Donne has expressed it in one of his sonnets.

"Death, be not proud, though some have called thee
 Mighty and dreadful, for thou art not so:
 For those whom thou think'st thou dost overthrow
 Die not, poor Death; nor yet canst thou kill me.
 From Rest and Sleep, which but thy picture be,
 Much pleasure, then from thee much more must flow;
 And soonest our best men with thee do go—
 Rest of their bones and souls' delivery!
 Thou'rt slave to fate, chance, kings, and desperate men,
 And dost with poison, war, and sickness dwell;
 And poppy or charms can make us sleep as well
 And better than thy stroke. Why swell'st thou then?
    One short sleep past, we awake eternally,
    And Death shall be no more: Death, thou shalt die!"

20 Archibald M. Hunter, "The Hope of Glory," *Interpretation*, April, 1954.
21 Geerhardus Vos, *Pauline Eschatology* (Eerdmans, 1952), p. 156.

VIII

THE DEFEAT
OF GOD'S ENEMIES

"God's affairs do not move backward but forward. The victory of living faith, in spite of various reverses in detail, yet viewed on the whole, strides irresistibly forward."[1] In these words Erich Sauer bears testimony to the thesis of these lectures: that the drama of redemption moves from a beginning in the creation and the story of the Fall, through a central climax in the tremendous events of the First Coming, to the denouement which the Second Coming will bring. We have seen that the Christian message makes sense only as it assumes a future stage, in which our Lord will complete what He has begun. We have pointed out four things which require this completion: His work among men, the spiritual maturity of His followers, the perfection of His Kingdom, and the defeat of the last enemy, Death. We will now describe other unfinished matters that need to be brought to a consummation by the denouement of the Parousia of Christ.

If the drama of redemption is to be brought to a logical finish, it must provide for the defeat, not only of death, but of every enemy of God. Those enemies are very real. From the temptation in Eden to the casting of Satan and his helpers into the lake of fire, as we read of it near the end of

1 Erich Sauer, *From Eternity to Eternity* (Eerdmans, 1954), p. 81.

Revelation, there runs through the whole history of the world the ominous undertone of opposition to the will and work of God. There are personalities of darkness which are the deadly enemies of the Light. There are principalities and powers of wickedness headed by that old serpent, the devil, who from the beginning in the Garden to the last uprising before the End, is determined to bring to naught the plan of God for man's eternal happiness in His Kingdom of blessedness. The powers of evil are continually attempting to negate all that God can do to work out His program of human redemption.

It is a part of the Good News of the Gospel that these enemies are already destined to defeat. The Messianic prophecies of the Old Testament made it clear that the Promised One should put all His enemies under His feet. When Jesus came He said one day, "I beheld Satan fallen as lightning from heaven."[2] The tense is past. The enemy is already vanquished. Paul wrote to the Colossians of the work of Christ, "having drawn the sting of all the powers ranged against us, He exposed them, shattered, empty and defeated, in His final glorious triumphant act!"[3]

The victory is already won. But while in a spiritual sense this is true, in its full sense it is only potential. In Hebrews we read that after His sacrifice Jesus sat down at the right hand of God "to wait until his enemies should be made a stool for his feet."[4] And Paul tells us that it is at the End when Christ "shall have abolished all rule and all authority and power." In Revelation we have the picture of the last stages of the struggle between the forces of good and evil, and of the victory of Christ. ". . . the Lamb shall

2 Luke 10:18.
3 Col. 2:15 (Phillips)
4 Heb. 10:13 (RSV).

overcome them, for he is Lord of lords, and King of kings; and they also shall overcome that are with him, called and chosen and faithful."[5]

Here we have again the pattern which we have seen before. Satan and his negative forces of evil already have judgment pronounced against them, but the judgment has not been carried out. "The powers of darkness . . . are unbroken in their actual effectiveness, and therefore set specific limits to all renewals of life which the Spirit of God achieves within history. . . . The advent of Christ in glory is primarily a negation of this negation, the destruction of these powers. . . ."[6] Of the outcome there is no doubt. But not until Christ comes again will we see it. We cannot bring it. It waits for divine action. "Christ's second appearing marks the end of all opposing rebellion . . . fixes the date for the execution of the condemnation of Satan and his hosts."[7] Whatever the seeming triumphs of evil now, we know the mysterious struggle in the world of spirits will end at the close of history in a complete and final triumph for our Lord. The course of events in the world "can be explained only in terms of the end toward which it is moving."[8]

Satan, then, is certain to come to ignominious defeat. He is working now on time which waits the Day of the Lord. The binding or restraint of which we read in several passages is for an interval only. But at the End he shall be cast into the lake of fire and be tormented for ever and ever."[9]

---

5 Rev. 17:14.
6 Emil Brunner, *Eternal Hope* (Westminster, 1954), p. 201.
7 R. B. Jones, *The Things Which Shall Be Hereafter* (Broadman, 1947), pp. 126 f.
8 Andre Trocme, *Politics of Repentance* (Fellowship Press, 1953), p. 47.
9 Rev. 20:10.

Another great power of evil of which we read is the Antichrist. Daniel told of a great personage of rebellion which he calls the little horn. Jesus spoke of false Christs and false prophets. Paul wrote of a "man of sin" who should arise just before the End, for he would be destroyed by the Revelation of Christ. John speaks of many antichrists, which are already here. And in Revelation 13 we read of a "beast" who has the same anti-God qualities as Paul's Man of Sin. One cannot be sure of the identity of the Antichrist. It may be only an attitude or ideology or institution which sets itself in opposition to God. More likely it is an individual who becomes an incarnation of blasphemous denial and opposition, a leader of forces opposing God. If a man, we do not know who the Antichrist is. There have been many foolish attempts to identify him: Nero, Mohammed, Cerinthus, Titus, Julian the Apostate, the Pope, Luther, Cromwell, Peter the Great, Napoleon, Mussolini, Nietzsche, Hitler, and Stalin have been among the guesses. The key for identification has often been the figure 666 from Revelation 13:18. By taking liberties with titles and spelling and numeral values of letters, a great many names can be made to add up to that figure. "Sir Thomas Browne [said] that the prophecies pertaining to the Antichrist, as explained in his day, were unsatisfactory, making too much of a present existing fulfillment, so that he concluded 'that Antichrist is the philosopher's stone in divinity.' "[10]

It will be best for us not to attempt to identify the Antichrist in some political or religious scene to which we are opposed, but to recognize how easy it is, in aspiring to fight for Christ, to fall into a philosophy or system that is op-

10 Geo. H. N. Peters, *The Theocratic Kingdom* (Kregel, 1952), II, p. 678.

posed to Christ. Then, if the Antichrist should arise in our day, we would be more likely to recognize him.

The most important thing in connection with our subject is to know that the success of Antichrist is short. The Lord Jesus, says Paul, at His coming will slay the Antichrist "with the breath of his mouth, and bring [him] to nought by the manifestation of his coming."[11] John says that the beast and the false prophet are in the lake of fire where Satan is cast. Thus after a brief period of rebellion and pompous claims this enemy of God shall be brought to an inglorious end. But it requires the bright light of the Parousia to expose and defeat him.

"Dr. John Brown, author of *Rab and His Friends,* tells how he once heard his revered father, Dr. Brown of Broughton Place, Edinburgh, preaching on the second psalm, 'Why do the heathen rage?' Pushing up his spectacles and laying aside his papers, Dr. Brown cried to the congregation, 'Where is Jesus now? And where are those priests and rulers now? Jesus is gone up, and has sat down, and shall forever sit, on the throne of the universe. Where they are, in heaven or in hell, I know not; but this I know, that wherever they be, they are, and shall forever be, at, or under His feet.' "[12]

11 II Thess. 2:8.
12 Quoted by Archibald M. Hunter, in "The Hope of Glory," *Interpretation,* April, 1954.

IX

THE JUDGMENT

A sixth need which requires the Coming of our Lord is the Judgment. When He comes, He will sit on the throne of His glory and all nations will be gathered before Him to be judged.[1] The Judgment, we recall, is an essential part of a minimal eschatology. Jesus will return; the dead will be raised; all men will be judged. The Scriptural evidence for these three propositions is unanswerable. Whatever else we believe or do not believe and preach about eschatology, if we accept the Scriptures as the Word of God we must accept the Parousia, the Resurrection, and the Judgment as the essential framework of the Last Things.

The root meaning of the Greek word usually used for judgment is separation. This meaning is used in several of the figures of the New Testament teaching: the sheep are separated from the goats, the wheat from the tares, the valuable fish from those of no value. While there are certain distinctions that are perfectly clear now, Jesus taught that the full differentiation must await a final judgment, when all the evidence is in. The wheat and the tares must grow together in the world until the harvest is ripe. Then the tares can be separated and burned. And Matthew 25 teaches that there will be surprises. Our human standards, apart from the light of God's insights, are very imperfect. Tillotson said, "We shall have two wonders in heaven; the one,

1 Matt. 25:31, 32.

how many come to be absent whom we expected to find there; the other, how many are there, whom we had no hope of meeting."[2]

There is much wrong in this world that requires righting, much confusion that needs to be put in order, much error that needs to be exposed by truth, many distortions of value that must be eliminated. History has a way of doing some of this. Schelling said that "the history of the world is the judgment of the world."[3] But as history clears some things up, it muddles others. Man, even collective man, cannot render righteous judgment. God must do that. "Just as the resurrection puts an end to death," says Brunner, "so judgment terminates the state of confusion and obscurity, of inconclusiveness. Judgment spells ultimate decision, and thus ultimate discrimination. . . . For the obscurity of the provisional stage, the condition in which the Lordship of Christ and that of Antichrist coexist, is intolerable. . . . That He permits the provisional stage of inconclusiveness to last so long is an indication of His patience."[4]

Jesus said that God had given all judgment unto Him.[5] Until He comes, therefore, to exercise that full judicial function, the judgment of the world must be very incomplete. Therefore the very close connection throughout the New Testament between judgment and the Second Coming.

New Testament teachings on the Judgment are a further revelation on the Old Testament foundations. The prophets from Joel to Malachi spoke of the Day of the Lord, "when God would intervene in human history to establish His

2 Quoted by Peters, *The Theocratic Kingdom* (Kregel, 1952), III, p. 276.

3 Quoted by Geo. L. Murray, *Millennial Studies* (Baker, 1948), p. 159.

4 Emil Brunner, *Eternal Hope* (Westminster, 1954), pp. 175 f.

5 John 5:22.

righteousness and to do away with sin."[6] Often it was a temporal happening, like a swarm of locusts or a foreign invasion. But always there are eschatological overtones. The prophets looked to the end of history when God would strike, and judgment would come. The people were prone to believe that they were God's chosen, and therefore the Day of the Lord would mean an established Kingdom for them, and judgment only upon their enemies. But "Amos . . . combated that delusion, declaring that the Day of Yahweh was also a day of judgment on sinful Israel."[7]

When in the New Testament Jesus Christ was recognized as the Lord who was to come, the phrase "the Day of the Lord" was appropriated as belonging to His era. Since with Christ the Messianic days had come, the author of Hebrews could say that "at the end of these days" God has spoken in His Son.[8] And Peter could say that Christ "was manifested at the end of the times."[9] Erich Sauer describes the situation well: "Christ is the final goal of the millenniums before the crisis of the ages. Therefore with His appearing the end age, that is, the goal age, had come—an organic united display of prophecy and fulfillment, of preparation and completion, which . . . led early apostolic thought to describe the whole New Testament time of salvation from the first appearing of Christ as 'End time,' as the 'last days. . . .' According to early Christian conviction the 'End time' began with the Incarnation of Christ."[10]

But though the last days had come, the last day had not. "The term 'day,'" says John C. Wenger, "is used about

6 Eric C. Rust, "Time and Eternity in Biblical Thought," *Theology Today*, October, 1953.

7 John Bright, *The Kingdom of God* (Abingdon, 1953), p. 145.

8 1:2.

9 I Pet. 1:20.

10 Erich Sauer, *From Eternity to Eternity* (Eerdmans, 1954), pp. 74, 75.

fifty times in the New Testament to refer to the coming of
Jesus."[11] It occurs alone or in such combinations as "day
of Christ," "day of the Lord," "that day," "day of judgment," "day of wrath," "day of redemption," and "last day."
To these expressions is attached the Old Testament connotation of a sudden, unexpected, inescapable, and imminent
coming of the Lord in judgment.

Because the Lord had already come, however, the one
who was to come was known to His own. Therefore the Day
was lovingly anticipated by those whose faith was in Him. In
fact, the day that commemorated the Resurrection came to
be called the "Lord's Day," a phrase which quite likely
looked forward as well as backward. John the Revelator
saw his panorama of the last days on "the Lord's day."[12]
This day spoke to believers of what Christ will yet do, in
view of what He has already done. And this was something
gloriously good, as well as ominously bad.

The chief connotation of judgment, however, continues to
be one of awful warning to those who have not known God
redemptively. The Messiah will burn the chaff which is
separated from the wheat.[13] As Judge He will render to
every man according to his deeds.[14] Those who have had
greater opportunity will receive greater condemnation.[15]
The judgment of God is something one may try to escape
but cannot.[16] There will be the pouring out of a stored-up
wrath.[17] God will judge the secrets people will hope they
have kept hidden.[18] On the unbelieving and the evildoer
He will pronounce a doom of eternal punishment.[19]

11 *Introduction to Theology* (Herald Press, 1954), p. 358.
12 Rev. 1:10.
13 Matt. 3:12.
14 Matt. 16:27.
15 Luke 20:47.
16 Rom. 2:3.
17 Rom. 2:5, 6.
18 Acts 2:16.
19 II Thess. 1:9.

Those who will be condemned in the Judgment will be assigned to hell. This awful fact has the undeniable support of Scripture. Surprisingly, most of the references to hell in the New Testament are made by Jesus Himself. The one who came to make it possible for us to spend eternity with Him in heaven was most explicit in His warnings that those who do not accept Him should suffer eternal torment in a Gehenna of fire. The outstanding thing about this eternal condition is separation from God. Those who have chosen to be godless shall remain godless. The only alternative to being eternally with God is being eternally with Satan in the lake of fire prepared for him. The fact that spirits, Satan and his angels, are being punished in hell shows that the nature of the punishment is such as can have effect upon spirits. On the other hand, one must remember that the unsaved are raised from the dead to be judged. It is resurrected bodies which go away into Gehenna—the whole man participating in the effect of his defiance of God. It will be a conscious existence—"everlasting self-accusation, with no chance or desire to try again."[20]

It is important to notice that immortality is not in itself salvation. The lost are immortal, but this brings only unending damnation. Through the centuries there have been those who could not bring themselves to believe in so dreadful a reality. But we have God's Word for it. That Word is this: "And these shall go away into eternal punishment: but the righteous into eternal life."[21] The same word, *aionios,* describes both the punishment and the life. Althaus says, "If 'eternal death' meant annihilation, God's judgment would be finite, limited by a saving, 'No more.' "[22] And

20 Gerrit Verkuyl, on Mark 9:48 in *Berkeley Version of the New Testament* (Zondervan, 1945).
21 Matt. 25:46.
22 Quoted by J. A. T. Robinson, *In the End God* (Clarke, 1950), p. 82.

to reason that somehow, sometime, God will include all in His redemptive purpose, is to reduce both salvation and judgment to meaninglessness. We must agree with Salmond: "In all love there is a fire, and the divine love is a just, holy, absolute love. A God incapable of the energy of wrath were a God incapable of the sovereignty of love."[23] Certainly one cannot get rid of hell simply by denying it. It is a matter of fact, not opinion. We may not understand it, but we do know how to keep from going there.

Heaven is just as real, thank God, as hell is. The Bible says still more about it. It is the place of the eternal habitation of the saved. It is a place of joy and comfort, of light and rest. Its Architect and its Builder is God. It is a better place than this earth. There will be no tears there, and no mourning; no pain, no hunger, no thirst. There we shall be with Christ; better than that, we shall be like Him, for at last we shall be perfectly conformed to His image. It will be a place of worship and of service. Sin will not enter heaven, nor will anyone that loves sin. There will be song and praise, and full ability and facility to explore the untracked riches of God's grace. Edward Wilson, before his death in the Antarctic, wrote to his wife, "All things I had hoped to do with you after this Expedition are as nothing now, but there are greater things for us to do in the world to come."[24]

John saw a new heaven, the holy city, new Jerusalem, coming down from God.[25] There is a heaven now, we know, where "as a forerunner Jesus entered for us."[26] In what sense the saved need to wait for the Resurrection in order

23 S. D. F. Salmond, *The Christian Doctrine of Immortality* (T. & T. Clark, Edinburgh, 1895), p. 648.

24 Quoted by D. T. Niles, *Preaching the Gospel of the Resurrection* (Westminster, 1954), p. 63.

25 Rev. 21:1, 2.

26 Heb. 6:20.

to enter into eternal blessedness we do not know. But it does seem that the heaven of our eternal abode will become ours only when Jesus comes again and makes all things new.

Let us take another look at Jesus in His function of judge. In John's Gospel we read that God has committed all judgment unto the Son.[27] In the Synoptics His judgment function seems to be in the future. But in John we read, "he that believeth not hath been judged already, because he hath not believed on the name of the only begotten Son of God."[28] Jesus did not come the first time primarily to be a judge; He came to be a savior. But His very presence constituted a scene of judgment. Men had to take some attitude toward Jesus. If they believed in Him, they were saved. If they rejected Him, they were condemned. Here we get the key fact concerning the judgment which Christ conducts. The determining factor is the attitude toward Him. Wherever He is, the court is in session. He who believes already has "passed out of death into life," and does not have to face judgment.[29] So when Jesus came the first time He was a judge; His presence inevitably involved that. In that sense the judgment continues throughout this age. Jesus has come, and the Gospel presents Him as the world's Saviour. The decision of every individual in his lifetime concerning Jesus determines his lot on the Judgment Day. Even now, we read, wrath is accumulating against the ungodly and the unbelievers. Here again we observe the tension which exists between that which already is and that which is to come.

But the judgment beginning at the First Advent and continuing through this era of the Gospel will be tremen-

27 John 5:22.
28 3:18.
29 John 5:24.

dously intensified and finalized when Jesus returns. Again
His presence will mean judgment. It is not a doomsday we
approach, but a Presence—a presence which will automat-
ically spell doom for those who have rejected or evaded
Him. The fact that men shall be judged by the deeds done
in the body is no argument against this. For men's deeds
are directly linked to their faith or their lack of faith. The
book of life and the book of works are cross-referenced.

So we see why Jesus must come again. There are multi-
tudes today who live as if there were no Christ. They have
heard false teachers say, or have made themselves believe,
that the Judgment is a medieval superstition. They have at
least postponed the Judgment to a date so far away that it
means nothing to them. The presence of Jesus at His Advent will mean something immediately. Then all the world
shall know that it is true that "we shall all stand before the
judgment-seat."[30]

This makes it possible too to understand in some degree
how the more or less simultaneous judgment of untold mil-
lions will be possible. John Wesley thought that the Great
Assize might last thousands of years. But we need not think
of the Great Judgment in terms of our court hearings. In
the presence of Christ all things are naked and open. We
remember how in His presence the accusers of the adulter-
ous woman saw their own sin plainly. " 'It comes to light'
. . . that is the essence of judgment. It is revealed—not for
God: for how could anything have been concealed from
Him?—but for ourselves. We shall stand naked and exposed
according to the truth of our being, with no concealing rai-
ment. No dossier, no protocol will be needed—the sole
decisive thing is the fact of manifestation."[31] In this sense

30 Rom. 14:10.
31 Emil Brunner, *op. cit.,* p. 176.

we shall judge ourselves, just as the evil-hearted old scribes and Pharisees did when Jesus stood silent before them. The books of our memories shall be opened when we stand in His holy presence. Though He will come the second time more particularly to judge, He will be the same person who came the first time. The same holiness and truth and love and understanding will be in evidence. He will simply be bringing to its full completion the judgment which He exercised before and is exercising now.

Will the saved be judged? Is their judgment completely past? Paul said that *we* shall all stand before the judgment seat, and that "each one of us shall give account of himself to God."[32] He told how our work, presumably as Christians, shall be tested by judgment and whatever proves worthless shall be burned.[33] "We must all be made manifest before the judgment-seat of Christ," he said, "that each one may receive the things done in the body . . . whether it be good or bad."[34] "No one can read Paul's letters without seeing how basic to his Christian belief was the thought of a Day of final reckoning, and how he lets the awe of it descend upon his heart to keep his conscience quick."[35] Surely the Christian life must be oriented toward the Day of Judgment.

Now it is difficult for us to understand how Paul, after all these centuries in bliss in the presence of Christ, should need to appear in judgment to learn whether he is saved or lost. But when one senses how important the quality of our life and work is, there seems yet abundant reason why we should in a future judgment appear for the scrutiny which will reveal the ultimate value of our lives. Even the Christian life is a probation which needs to be tested and

32 Rom. 14:10, 12.
33 I Cor. 3:13-15.
34 II Cor. 5:10.
35 Archibald M. Hunter, "The Hope of Glory," *Interpretation*, April, 1954.

approved. "The believer is not allowed, any more than the unbeliever, to enter his final destiny with a false estimate of himself."[36] But John speaks of having "complete confidence on the Day of Judgment."[37] That may be what we call assurance of salvation. But even such boldness does not preclude the moral and spiritual sensitivity which Pascal expressed in these words: ". . . I shall find myself entirely separated from the world, stripped naked of all things, standing alone before Thee, to answer to Thy justice concerning all the motions of my thought and spirit."[38] Our Lord always reserves the right to an accounting. The attitude of the servant will deteriorate if he forgets that.

Bernard of Cluny, of the twelfth century, calls us to prepare for the coming of the Judge and the Judgment:

> "The world is very evil;
>   The times are waxing late;
>   Be sober and keep vigil,
>   The Judge is at the gate:
>   The Judge that comes in mercy,
>   The Judge that comes in might,
>   To terminate the evil,
>   To diadem the right."

36 T. A. Kantonen, *The Christian Hope* (Muhlenberg, 1954), p. 105.
37 I John 4:17 (Weymouth).
38 Quoted by T. F. Glasson, *His Appearing and His Kingdom* (Epworth, 1953), p. 83.

X

THE TRIUMPH
OF THE CHURCH

We turn to a seventh reason why Christ must come again. He must come to bring final triumph to His body, the church. The word *ecclesia,* which is translated *church* in the New Testament, was used in the Septuagint to mean the whole assembly of the people. In that sense Stephen used it in Acts 7:38 with reference to the assembly of Israel. No doubt this is its primary meaning when it is applied to the New Testament believers: it is the whole people of God. Phillips translates I Peter 2:9, "all the old titles of God's People now belong to you."[1] It is the word Jesus applied to His followers when during His ministry the lines were being drawn between those who believed and those who did not. He spoke of building a church.[2]

The church had its beginning in those astounding events of Calvary and Easter and Pentecost which we have called the climax of all history. After that the church is either the fellowship of believers in some city or meeting in somebody's house, or it is the mystical body of those everywhere who are truly Christ's, united to Him in a genuine spiritual attachment. The church is the assembly of the first-born, enrolled in heaven,[3] but functioning upon the earth. It be-

1 J. B. Phillips, *Letters to Young Churches* (Macmillan, 1948).
2 Matt. 6:18.
3 Heb. 12:23.

longs to the New Age, brought in with Christ, but coexisting with "this age" of the present world. It experiences the tension of living by the principles of a coming age in an environment which loves the present age. It is commanded not to be conformed to this age, not to be wise according to the standards of this age. It lives simultaneously "in Christ" and "at Ephesus."[4] In an age which is passing away it affirms the things that are eternal. "The church is not *in patria* but *in via*."[5] It is a pilgrim church, journeying through a world in which it is not at home.

The church will, of course, be a participator in the eternal Kingdom. Paul prays that God may have glory in the church forever.[6] But the earthly functions of the church, such as the administration of baptism and the Lord's Supper, the preaching of the Gospel to the lost, the exemplification of righteous living in an evil world, the martyrdom of suffering which witnessing often involves, the discipline by which the church is kept pure—these will be a thing of the past after the Parousia of our Lord. The church, therefore, has something of an interim character. The age of the church "lies between the perfect tense of the resurrection and the future tense of ultimate fulfillment."[7] These two events—the Resurrection and the Parousia—are the framework of the Church Age. God has sent a Saviour, who lives and reigns—of this the church witnesses. He will send Him again, to complete and fulfill and to "deliver us out of this present evil age"[8]—this the church lovingly anticipates.

The church on earth is the affianced bride of Christ. The Second Coming is the time of the marriage. Christ will re-

---

4 Eph. 1:1.
5 K. E. Skydsgaard, "Kingdom of God and Church," *Scottish Journal of Theology*, December, 1951.
6 Eph. 3:21.
7 K. E. Skydsgaard, *op. cit.*   8 Gal. 1:4.

joice in the purity and beauty of His bride. The marriage supper of the Lamb is a symbol of the joyous and uninterrupted fellowship which will follow the Parousia. Naturally the period of waiting is a time of loving anticipation. It is not impatient waiting, for the church is sure that "journeys end in lovers meeting." The present time of affianced love is a constant joy. The length of time the bride must wait is not important. As Jacob's seven years of service seemed only a few days because of the love which he had for Rachel,[9] so the bride and the Bridegroom are not chiefly concerned about the time involved, but rather in the event itself. Until Christ comes, His church will love His appearing.[10]

The church now is composed of extremely imperfect men. On the other side of the Parousia, that which is perfect will have come. Now we have only tasted "the powers of the age to come"[11]; then we shall realize those powers in their fullness. Now we are "in Christ," but then we shall be "with Christ." Now we serve Him in all the limitations of "the body of our humiliation"[12]; then we shall be like His "glorious body." With all its blessings and joy, the church is only "a foretaste and adumbration of the Kingdom of God."[13]

There is no doubt justification for some of the present divisions in the church. Truth is often served in denominational emphases. But no one thinks that these divisions will survive the advent of Christ. At the end of history Christ will accomplish a unity that we could not achieve. He will gather His whole church into one, as His judgment melts away the insufficient causes which have divided; as, in fact,

9 Gen. 29:20.
10 II Tim. 4:8.
11 Heb. 6:5.
12 Phil. 3:21.
13 Emil Brunner, *Eternal Hope* (Westminster, 1954), p. 166.

He reveals that some who speak His name do not belong to Him at all.

As a corrective to selfish ambitions for an individual salvation it is important to get the concept of corporate salvation. It is true that each person stands alone in his accountability to God. But "what the New Testament has to say about the future of each of us is indissolubly bound up with our membership, in Christ, with one another. Our hope is corporate; it is nothing else than that in Christ all things in heaven and earth should be reconciled, summed up. It is, therefore, unthinkable that any individual should share in that salvation except in its totality which includes all that are Christ's."[14] And so the church, as a body to be eternally redeemed in the same fellowship which the members knew on earth, only vastly enriched, is a part of our glorious prospect, to be realized when our Lord comes. Thus the people of God are seen to be the people of His agelong purpose, the goal-people who play their part in the consummation of all the ages.

One other blessing which will come to God's people at the Second Advent is the reward which He gives for faithful service. We may think we do not serve for reward, but God is not a miserly Master. "The web of Biblical eschatology is shot through with the strand of reward."[15] A reward has been promised, a great reward,[16] a crown of life and glory.[17] Credits get strangely confused among us. But when the Lord comes He will apportion the rewards with justice and truth. His accounting will set many things right that are now wrong.

14 J. E. L. Newbigin, *Missions Under the Cross* (Friendship Press, 1953), p. 110.

15 Geerhardus Vos, *Pauline Eschatology* (Eerdmans, 1952), p. 64.

16 Luke 6:23.

17 Rev. 2:10; I Pet. 5:4.

XI

GOD'S PURPOSES FOR THE EARTH

The eighth and last need for Christ's Parousia is that He may complete His purpose for the world. God created the world and all that is in it. In this He had a purpose. The Eternal Son participated in this creation. He was in the beginning with God.[1] He is the Alpha. He became intimately connected with affairs on the earth when as incarnate God He became the center of all history, the point of reference for all that preceded and all that followed. Christianity is historically based, finding its development and its meaning in the stream of history. It is concerned with what has happened, what is happening, and what will happen. Just as Christ is concerned with the beginning of this world, with the course of history through the centuries, so He is concerned with its end. He must be the Omega as well as the Alpha and all the alphabet between. "The Will of God revealed to us in Jesus Christ as the world-ground and the world-origin is also disclosed to us in Him as the world-goal and the world-end,"[2] says Emil Brunner, and continues, "The creation is understood in the light of its end, and the end for which the world was created can be no other than the goal of history: 'Christ, the hope of glory.'"[3]

1 John 1:2, 3.
2 Emil Brunner, *Eternal Hope* (Westminster, 1954), p. 187.
3 *Ibid.*, p. 189.

History must be understood in terms of time and place. The time of history is the line from the beginning to the end. The time line has its beginning in Christ in God. It must have an end that is just as historical as its beginning. And that end, the Scriptures tell us, is also in Christ in God. If there had been any doubt concerning whom the time line belonged to, that doubt was fully dissolved when Christ became man and took His place in the unfolding events of history. The process is now His, and the goal will be His. The time line must be completed; this age must give way to the age that is to come. But all this must occur in the kind of sequence which history knows. 'To cut out the historical element from the Christian creed is to cut out the core of the Christian revelation and the heart of the Christian good news."[4]

History has meaning only when it is seen as the working out of the purpose of God. That purpose is the production of the image of God in man, to the glory of God. The theme of history centers around the attempts of the Enemy to defeat that purpose, and the action of God for its accomplishment through Christ. There is a goal which God has set and thus has given a direction to history. And because there is a goal, "there is a necessary structure and order in history which is divinely ordained. There is a certain flexibility, to be sure, in this divine order, brought about by the response of faith on the part of man, but God still knows the beginning and the end and no human agency will obstruct His holy purpose."[5]

Struggling to find its own way through the centuries, history often seems to be "the story of an ever-increasing cos-

---

4 J. E. Fison, *The Christian Hope* (Longmans, 1954), p. 2.

5 Charles T. Fritch, "Message of Apocalyptic for Today," *Theology Today*, October, 1953.

mos creating ever-increasing possibilities of chaos."[6] But God will not leave history to itself. He entered the stream of history in the Incarnation and did those mighty deeds which brought in a new era. And to those struggling with the dilemmas and contradictions of our time, all but overwhelmed by what Byron called the "deep melancholy of history," He speaks the certain word that He will intervene again, and by that eschatological intervention bring order out of chaos and bring history to its intended goal. The confusion of a Christ-rejecting society will give way to the ordered meaning of a redeemed society where Christ is finally supreme.

So-called secular history can record happenings, but has great difficulty in revealing a goal or purpose. A competent historian, Karl Jaspers, in *The Origin and Goal of History*, says, "God's passage through history became visible . . . in the succession of His acts running from creation, *via* expulsion from Paradise, announcement of His will through the prophets, redemption through His appearance in person at the turning point of the ages, to the end in the anticipated Last Judgment, in which everything has its place. A series of fundamental principles of human existence made their appearance which, apprehended in their depths, taught what truly is and happens."[7] The course of history must be seen as a whole, with the perspective which revelation has given us. "The end is placed in the light of the beginning, and all intermediate developments are construed with reference to the . . . *terminus ad quem*. Eschatology," says Vos, "yields *ipso facto* a philosophy of history."[8] And Davidson has said, "Prophecy is history become conscious—history ex-

6 Quoted by J. E. Fison, *op. cit.*, p. 65.

7 *The Origin and Goal of History* (Yale, 1953), p. 259.

8 Geerhardus Vos, *Pauline Eschatology* (Eerdmans, 1953), p. 61.

pressing its own meaning."[9] A further word from Emil Brunner is pertinent here. "Just as the one origin in creation, so the one redemption and fulfillment as the goal of history gathers the destinies of nations into a comprehensive unity. In this sense it may well be said that the conception of world history is Christian in origin and subsists through Christian faith."[10]

Apart from the Christian hope in eschatology, history may fill us with gloom. Max Weber said that world history resembles a street paved by the devil with destroyed values.[11] Apart from the promise and prospect of divine intervention the drama of history is a tragedy, stark and well-nigh hopeless. It is the purpose of God, and the assurance that that purpose will not fail, which turns the drama into a comedy of triumphant love. When Christ was born into the world, it became apparent that God would not rest until He had indeed turned tragedy into comedy, that is, a drama which ends in a happy tone.

But only God can do it. Paul Peachey says, ". . . The incongruities of human existence and of the social order can reach final solution only as the regenerative process comes to maturity eschatologically."[12] The state cannot do it. All political solutions are only preliminary and may create new problems. The church cannot do it; at least, there does not seem to be one word in the New Testament which would indicate that the church will be able to "bring in the Kingdom." No, "only God can fulfill the purpose of history. The New Jerusalem comes down from above."[13] Social evolution

9 A. B. Davidson, *Old Testament Prophecy* (Clark, 1912), p. 98.

10 *Op. cit.*, p. 39.

11 Quoted by Karl Jaspers, *op. cit.*, p. 270.

12 "Toward an Understanding of the Decline of the West," *Concern*, June, 1954, p. 37.

13 T. F. Torrance, "Modern Eschatological Debate," *Evangelical Quarterly*, October, 1953.

leaves us disappointed; social revolution leaves us frightened. We can hope in no one but God.

What of the future of this earth? When we speak of the End, do we understand that this earth which God created and upon which we exist, this earth to which Christ came and where He performed the great work of eternal redemption, shall vanish into nothingness? Does complete redemption involve only the whole man, body and soul, or is there also to be a cosmic redemption, so that the whole of God's creation may be finally transformed to serve its glorious creation purpose? Does God's judgment of wicked men include also the utter destruction of this earth as hopelessly involved in the sin of man? Does this earth belong to a limited time order which shall serve its purpose and then be annihilated while God carries out His program for redeemed man in some otherworldly sphere?

Many Christians have understood the Bible to teach that when the course of events associated with the Parousia is finished, then God will annihilate this earth. The phrase which Jesus used, "the end of the world,"[14] seemed to imply that. "Heaven and earth shall pass away," He said, "but my words shall not pass away."[15] "The world passeth away, and the lust thereof," said John.[16] "The first heaven and the first earth are passed away . . . the first things are passed away," are the words of the Revelator.[17] And Peter tells of the heavens passing away with a great noise, of the elements being dissolved and melting, of the earth being burned up.[18] Hebrews, using a figure from the Old Testament prophets, speaks of God's shaking the earth, so that the things which cannot be shaken, or destroyed, may remain.[19]

14 Matt. 13:39.
15 Matt. 24:35.
16 I John 2:17.
17 Rev. 21:1, 4.
18 II Pet. 3:10-12.
19 Heb. 12:26, 27.

There was a time when the utter destruction of the earth
seemed ridiculous to scientifically minded pople. Today it
is the scientists and historians who are telling us how possible it is for a technological civilization to destroy the planet
upon which it exists. Karl Jaspers says, "Technology . . .
increases the peril beyond all measure, to the point at
which we contemplate the possibility of pulverizing the
globe in space . . . . With the atom bomb, a piece of solar
substance has been brought to the earth. The same thing
happens to it on the surface of the earth which has hitherto
happened only in the sun . . . . It is uncertain beyond what
dividing-line the explosion will lay hold on further elements
and terrestrial matter as a whole, like a conflagration. The
whole globe would explode, whether intentionally or unin-
tentionally. Then our solar system would be temporarily
lit up, a *nova* would have appeared in space."[20] This sounds
a great deal like Peter's description. Arnold J. Toynbee, the
great British historian, tells us that "science has placed in
human hands the power to destroy life on earth."[21] Some
of our scientists are being driven by politicians to do tasks
which they shrink from because they realize the awful possibilities. Man is now playing with forces that he knows may
get beyond his control. And God may use the sinful folly
of men to bring about the conflagration of judgment which
Peter describes.

However, let us not get the idea that the prophesied end
is only the result of human tampering with the elemental
forces of the universe. Edmund Schlink has said, "There is
an essential difference . . . between the fears of modern man
and the New Testament proclamation of the end of the
world. . . . In the New Testament the calamities of the last

20 *Op. cit.*, pp. 208 f.
21 "A Turning Point in Man's Destiny." *New York Times,* Dec. 26, 1954.

days are not merely human misdoings nor are they the consequence of human frailty. They are rather the activity of God Himself. In the New Testament it is God who will bring the end of the world. It is from God's throne that the orders go out, that send the apocalyptic riders over the earth . . . . The end of the world is the day of divine judgment."[22] God uses men, but He is not dependent upon them. When the time comes to break the earth asunder, He will not be lacking in means to do it. The God who spoke the world into existence could speak it out of existence again if that is what He chose to do.

But annihilation need not be His purpose. Here we must be careful not to go beyond revelation, either in arguing for annihilation or against it. Brunner says, "World-consummation as the goal of redemption through Jesus Christ, and as the cosmic scope of the completion of human history in the Kingdom of God, is only slightly indicated in the New Testament witness. The cosmic element in Scripture is always only the framework and the setting of the history of mankind as a whole. Of course we hear of 'a new heaven and a new earth.' But nothing is said as to what and in what manner this new heaven and new earth are to be, except that 'righteousness will dwell there.' "[23]

It should be made clear, however, that annihilation of the earth is not clearly taught in the Scriptures. The word *parerchomai* which is translated "pass away" does not mean annihilate. Culver says, "The meaning is rather to pass from one position in time or space to another. And even granting the most destructive ideas as the meanings of *luthestai* (be dissolved) and *katakaesetai* (be burned up, if we adopt the Textus Receptus), the words certainly do not

22 "Christ—the Hope of the World," *Christian Century*, Aug. 25, 1954.
23 Emil Brunner, *op. cit.*, pp. 202 f.

describe annihilation."[24] Peter speaks of two world judgments: one by water, the Flood, in which the world "perished" but was obviously not annihilated; and one by fire, in which the world shall be burned up, but not necessarily annihilated.

In any case, we know there is to be a new heaven and a new earth, according to Peter and John the Revelator. This could be a new creation, but it seems more likely to be a renovation of the present earth to serve the purposes of God after the end of this age. Jesus spoke of a "regeneration" in connection with the Judgment.[25] And Peter told of the restitution, or restoration, of all things.[26] Thayer's Lexicon says concerning the word "regeneration" which Jesus used, "that signal and glorious change of all things (in heaven and earth) for the better, that restoration of the primal and perfect condition of things which existed before the fall of our first parents, which the Jews looked for in connection with the advent of the Messiah, and which the primitive Christians expected in connection with the visible return of Jesus from heaven."[27]

There is other Scriptural support of the hope for cosmic regeneration. Paul says that "all nature is expectantly waiting for the unveiling of the sons of God," and that "even nature itself" is to "be set free from its bondage to decay, so as to share the glorious freedom of God's children."[28] Here is the final stage of God's creative act, when at last God's purposes in the creation will be fully realized. Better than annihilating the earth will be regenerating it. Says Kantonen, ". . . so the Kingdom will penetrate the world

24 Robert D. Culver, *Daniel and the Latter Days* (Revell, 1954), p. 184.
25 Matt. 19:28.
26 Acts 3:21.
27 Quoted by Culver, *op. cit.*, p. 188.
28 Rom. 8:19, 21 (Williams).

and transform it from within . . . . Jesus describes a 'regeneration' of the world . . . a glimmer of the hope that mankind as a whole would experience something of that transformation from self-centeredness to God-centeredness which regeneration implies in the lives of individuals."[29]

Many of the best commentators agree with this interpretation. Lenski, for example, says, on II Peter 3, "The heavens and the earth shall be renovated, renewed, purified, made perfect." Salmond says, "Creation is linked with man, involved in the consequences of his failure, but sharer also with him in the glory that is to be revealed. Nature is in sympathy with man, one with him in the doom, but one with him also in the redemption . . . . Men's world . . . carries in its constitution and on its face the intimation of its lapse from its original purpose, but also the token that this is not a condition to which it shall be bound forever. The presage is in it of a return to its primal condition. . . . Creation is burdened with a purposelessness which cannot be original to it, with a decay and a limitation which cannot be its primal law. . . . The attitude of creation is not that of final acquiescence, but that of waiting expectation. It has the light of better things on it, and points with prophetic finger to a change, a removal of the burden, a reversal of the doom, an abolition of the curse. The destiny to which it looks is emancipation. . . . When Christ returns and completes the adoption, the world itself shall step forth from its prisonhouse and share in the glorious freedom of the sons of God."[30]

It seems reasonable that just as the power of Satan in death shall be broken as our bodies are raised and fitted for our eternal dwelling, so the earth should not be left to

29 *Op. cit.*, p. 52.
30 *Christian Doctrine of Immortality* (T. & T. Clark, 1895), pp. 556 f.

the power of the Enemy, but should also be prepared for eternal and blessed purposes. We may not wish to go so far as does Geerhardus Vos and say that "the central abode of the redeemed will be in heaven, although the renewed earth will remain accessible to them and a part of the inheritance."[31] But in view of the purpose of God in creation, His power to accomplish His purposes, the far-reaching effects of redemption in body as well as in soul, and the completeness of the sovereignty which He shall establish, such a conclusion seems at least possible. The evil which entered the world through the Fall affected the whole order. When Christ came to overcome that evil He gave the deathblow to it, in all its areas. Although mankind is the center of the redemptive program, it seems most reasonable that it should have a wider, cosmic scope. And this fits the few references on the point by Jesus and the apostles. The fact that the new heaven and the new earth are mentioned together suggests that in the eternal ages they shall be united in "one great realm of righteousness."[32] This cosmic goal is a part of the consummation, which will be wrought by Christ's Second Coming. We are blessed with the prospect that the world will not continue forever under the curse of sin.

We have now come to the end of our brief listing of the reasons why Christ must come to earth a second time. The end-times in which we live had their beginning in the incarnation of Christ. For then He came to defeat the work of Satan, who as the enemy of God had infected the earth and its inhabitants with sin. Christ brought redemption to lost men and established the reign of righteousness in the earth.

---

31 Art. "Eschatology," *International Standard Bible Encyclopedia*, II, p. 991.

32 Footnote on Rev. 21:1 in *Berkeley Version of the New Testament* (Zondervan, 1945).

But the New Age which He thus inaugurated did not immediately and completely displace the Old Age. The work which He began in and for men needed to be carried on in the world until He should come back again, as He promised to do. Meanwhile the opposition of Satan continues, and there is a tension between what has already been done and that which is yet to do. This is a period of overlapping: the work of Christ has been begun but the opposing work of Satan has not been ended. Believers in Christ are living in the power of what Christ has already done for their eternal redemption, but they are waiting for the completion of that redemption, which can come only when Christ returns in glory. The drama of redemption which had its beginning at the creation passed its mid-point climax in Christ's incarnational ministry. It now needs to be carried on to its denouement in the Parousia and all that will take place in connection with it.

In this denouement all that is partial and provisional in the mediatorial work of Christ will be brought to fulfillment and completion. The full potential of present spiritual experience will be realized. The Kingdom of God, now real but hidden, will be manifested in its full power and glory. There will be full deliverance from all enemies, including the last one, Death. Satan and all his forces will be brought to final discomfiture and punishment. The Judgment will bring full moral discernment and the separation of good and bad. The church, the interim body of Christ, will be brought into glory and blessing in the eternal Kingdom, united forever to the Lord Jesus. And the complete purpose of the creation will be realized in a new heaven and new earth.

But all this waits for the End. "Belief in eschatology," says Lesslie Newbigin, "without belief in a real End is like belief in religion without belief in God."[33] A time line which has use for God only vertically at any given point, but goes forward into a vague and indefinite future, represents a kind of atheism. To be self-revealing, God must reveal enough of the future to give His own guidance and hope. And having revealed it, He must turn promise and hope into real experience. This we believe He will do.

It is only in the completion of His plan and purpose that God will be fully revealed and fully vindicated. Then shall be demonstrated the ultimate of His majesty, power, and goodness. Then shall all His creatures be in a position to give Him the glory and praise which is His due. Then shall the character, the accomplishment, and the love of the Son of God be fully evident, verifying all the claims He made during His first advent. Then shall the life of the Spirit find unhindered functioning in the spiritual bodies of the heavenly realm. Then shall be summed up all that heaven and earth can say and do to justify the ways of God in the never-flagging, never-dying tribute: "Unto him that sitteth on the throne, and unto the Lamb, be the blessing, and the honor, and the glory, and the dominion, for ever and ever. Amen."[34]

33 Quoted by Archibald M. Hunter, *op. cit.*
34 Rev. 5:13, 14.

PART III

WATCH THEREFORE

XII

WAITING
FOR THE PAROUSIA

To arrive at an understanding of the Christian hope one must ask and find the Scriptural answer to two questions. The first is, What has God done? The second is, What has God promised? All that God may yet do is inseparably bound up with what He has already done. The drama of God's program for the world and for men unfolds logically. There is a real sequence between the former and latter deeds. The climax is the proper development of the beginning, and the denouement is in perfect accord with the intimations of the climax.

And what has God done? He created the universe in its incomprehensible magnitude and spendor. He made this earth to be the home of the human race and to be the stage of redemption. He created man in His own image, and planned that man should have eternal fellowship with Him. When man fell into sin God put into motion the sequence of divine deeds which could redeem and restore him. He revealed Himself to man in the law and the prophets. He gave His promise of a Messiah who should be both Saviour and Lord. In the fullness of time this Saviour became incarnate man upon this earth; revealing divine love and righteousness, dying an atoning death, rising victorious over all enemies, setting up the reign of God in the hearts and lives of all who believed in Him, inaugurating the New Messianic Age, building a church upon the earth, and sending the Holy Spirit to dwell within His own. So tremendous is the accomplishment of Christ in His first advent, so far-reaching the effects of those mighty acts, that the Incarnation, the death on Calvary, the Easter resurrection, and the Pentecost outpouring are rightly thought of as the climax of the ages. Here God entered human history to transform and redeem it. He showed Himself to be the Lord of history as He demonstrated His will to righteousness, and His power to make that will prevail. He did not allow sin and death to triumph, but intervened to save His creation from the ruin that the Enemy intended. The work of Christ became effective to save lost men from the deadly consequences of their rebellion against the will and purpose of God. The Christian Gospel looks back to something done by God for sinners who could do nothing for themselves. Therefore it is the Good News.

Now the second question, What has God promised? For even in the doing of the deeds which wrought the Gospel, He promised yet other deeds. Implicit in the things which were done were other things yet to be done. The salvation accomplished spoke of a salvation yet to be completed. The work of Christ was perfect but not complete. There are many beginnings which need to be brought to a final and triumphant ending. The plot of the divine drama must be unfolded to the very End.

Our Gospel is a Gospel of promise. That idea and that word abounds in the New Testament. Nearly forty passages contain this word "promise." And they are central, conspicuous passages, so that one may say that all New Testament teaching is built around promise and its fulfillment. The First Advent was rich in its fulfillment of Old Testament promise. But the promise goes beyond that

Advent to another Coming in which the great plan which
God has devised for His creation will be brought into complete realization. God has promised the Denouement, the
second appearing upon earth of the Lord and Saviour Jesus Christ. In this second appearing He will finish all that
has been left incomplete, will end the tensions of the present era in which the New Age and the Old Age are coexisting, although in intrinsic opposition to each other. We
have seen in how many ways our present situation, glorious
as it is in God's rich provision for us, requires the second
coming of Christ in order that God's promised purposes
may be brought into complete fulfillment.

Jesus promised that He would come again. All the writing apostles promised that Jesus would come. For almost
two thousand years the church of Christ has been await-
ing the fulfillment of these promises. Peter tells us that
"the Lord is not slow in fulfilling His promise."[1] But it
sometimes seems that He is. We are a waiting church,
"waiting for the revelation of our Lord Jesus Christ." Like
the Thessalonians we "wait for his Son from heaven."[2] We
need to be reminded that this is the normal attitude of the
church all through the present era—watchful waiting for
One who will surely come, but who has not yet come. The
time is long, in any concept of time with which we are familiar. We need to guard against impatience on the one
hand, and forgetfulness on the other.

What do we wait for? We wait, of course, for a Person.
But the event grows out of the Person. We wait for the
Coming of a Person. The Person is Christ; the Coming
throughout these lectures we have called the Parousia. This
is a Greek noun which means "coming." It occurs in the

1 II Pet. 3:9 (Weymouth).
2 I Thess. 1:10.

New Testament to refer to the coming of Paul and Stepha-
nas, as well as of Christ. But always when used of Christ it
seems to refer to His final Coming in glory. And so to have
a word that refers to that great event alone it is a growing
practice to bring Parousia over into the English vocabulary.
It really means "presence." It was in the East a technical
expression for the arrival or the visit of the king or the
emperor. The corresponding Latin word, with the same
connotation, was *Advent,* which the Latin Christians took
over as a translation of Parousia.[3] Every New Testament
writer refers to the doctrine of the Parousia. The Old
Testament, of course, makes no mention of the Parousia
in the New Testament sense, but the essential idea is in
Zechariah 9:9: "Behold, thy king cometh unto thee."

Parousia is a better term than "second coming," for it is
Scriptural, as "second coming" is not. Hebrews does tell us
that Christ shall appear a second time.[4] We use the term
"second coming" to contrast it with the first coming, but
it would be fortunate if Parousia, with all its rich Scriptural
connotation, could come into common use. The term means
"arrival," not "return." For that reason also "second coming" may give a wrong idea.[5]

The emphasis must be on His coming to us, not our going to Him. Just as the Incarnation was a coming, God
with us, so the Parousia will be a coming. We sometimes
describe death as going to be with the Lord. We image the
body staying here and the soul going somewhere else, where
the Lord is. For that reason death cannot be the Parousia.
This is not some place to go. It is Someone to come. The

3 Deissman, *Light from the Ancient East,* quoted by Alexander Reese,
The Approaching Advent of Christ (Marshall, Morgan, and Scott, 1937),
pp. 143 f.
4 Heb. 9:28.
5 Geerhardus Vos, *Pauline Eschatology* (Eerdmans, 1952), p. 75.

initiative, the approach is His, not ours. He comes to us on earth; we do not go to Him in heaven. The choice of time and the prescription of manner is His, not ours. *We wait* until *He comes.*

The Parousia is the key to the whole eschatological future. It opens the door to the whole scheme of reality which is beyond history. It brings the Resurrection and the Judgment, which together with the Parousia are the completion of redemption; it brings the eternal Kingdom, the new heaven and new earth, the end of time, the glory of the Presence. The Parousia, says Vos, "is a point of eventuation, not a series of successive events. . . . It designates *the Momentous event. . . .* To conceive of Paul focusing his mind on any phase of relative consummation, and as tying up to this the term Parousia inevitably would involve his relegating the eternal things to a rank of secondary importance."[6] So we are not waiting specifically for the Resurrection, or the Judgment, or the Kingdom. We await the Parousia. When Christ comes He will bring with Him every effect that His Presence will involve. The program comes with the Program Maker. The Parousia is the inauguration of all that is involved in the Consummation. It looks forward to the age that is to come. It is the End only in being the end of this age. It is the opening, the grand entrance, into all that is in store in the ages of the ages, both for the saved individual and the saved society. It "links this world to the next," not by some slow process of development, but by a sudden, catastrophic meeting. The old comes to an end in a moment because the new is brought in by His Parousia. The narrow and limited pathway of this life at some unexpected point opens up into the

6 *Ibid.,* p. 76.

infinite, unimaginable prospects of the Coming Age. That point is the Parousia, for which we wait.

Because the Parousia is central to all eschatology, and because eschatology is an integral part of all theology, "it is impossible to cut the expectation of the Parousia entirely out of New Testament Christianity without destroying an integral part of it. 'He shall come again to judge the quick and the dead' stands securely in the church's creeds."[7] Brunner insists that "to try to boggle at [the Parousia] means to try to boggle at the foundation of the faith; to smash the cornerstone by which all coheres and apart from which all falls to pieces. Faith in Jesus Christ without expectation of His Parousia is a voucher that is never redeemed, a promise that is not seriously meant. A Christian faith without expectation of the Parousia is like a ladder which leads to nowhere but ends in the void."[8]

Concerning the manner of the Parousia there is little revealed. Jesus said that He would come on the clouds of heaven with power and great glory. The angels sent to gather the elect would be sent with the great sound of a trumpet.[9] At the Ascension the two in white apparel said Jesus would come in like manner as they had seen Him go.[10] Paul wrote to both the Corinthians and the Thessalonians of the trumpet sound.[11] If one remembers the Old Testament use of the trumpet, this eschatological trumpet peal is both ominous of judgment and a call to participate in the Jubilee of the New Age. Paul also writes of the shout of the archangel. Since Christ is to come in glory, we associate with that a brightness and light, as was illustrated

7 J. A. T. Robinson, *In the End God* (Clarke, 1950), p. 51.
8 Emil Brunner, *Eternal Hope* (Westminster, 1954), pp. 138 f.
9 Matt. 24:30, 31.
10 Acts 1:11.
11 I Cor. 15:52; I Thess. 4:16.

by the Transfiguration. Lange says, "The Parousia of
Christ is the Epiphany of God, in brilliancy like the most
precious jewel."[12]

One need not insist on imaging all this too clearly. Divine action is hard to put into human speech. It is super-
natural, and so unimaginable. It is idle, for instance, to ask
how a trumpet sound could be heard around the world,
and puerile to suggest that the devices of radio and tele-
vision may be used. What about the people who are not
tuned in? The Parousia as described in the Scriptures is
no more improbable than a virgin birth and a resurrection
from the grave. We can accept the fact and leave the im-
plementation to God. We may be sure there will be surprises. "No eschatology which eliminates . . . surprise can
claim for one moment to be Biblical,"[13] says Fison.

When will He come? Here we are certain of only one
thing, that no man knows. Jesus told His disciples, "But
of that day and hour knoweth no one, not even the angels
of heaven, neither the Son, but the Father only."[14] And
after His resurrection He said, "It is not for you to know
times or seasons, which the Father hath set within his own
authority."[15] It is one of the wonders of the history of eschatology, that in spite of this clear warning that no one on
earth could know anything about it, students of prophecy
from New Testament times to this have become preoccupied
with matters of chronology and date-setting, often to the
neglect of much more important details of eschatology.
"Any attempts to fix, even roughly and by implication, the
date of the End are false to that strand of the New Testa-

12 Quoted by Geo. H. N. Peters, *Theocratic Kingdom* (Kregel, 1952), III,
p. 313.
13 J. E. Fison, *The Christian Hope* (Longmans, 1954), p. 65.
14 Matt. 24:36.
15 Acts 1:7.

ment which makes of the End both in content and in timing a surprise," says David M. Paton.[16] In fact, it seems almost vulgar and irreverent to be stirring around in an area which God has said is secret with Him. Our Lord did not indicate any curiosity in this matter at all. He simply said He would come when He was not expected. When His disciples asked curious questions about the times and the seasons, He rebuked them. The apostles all taught the imminence of the Coming, but never attempted to set the time. Paul often intimated that Christ might come before his death, but he never said He would.

A little survey of the dismal and extensive history of date-setting ought to warn us against saying or writing things that may sound foolish down the years.

Already in apostolic times there were those who felt that the Parousia had been so long delayed that it probably would never come.[17] In the third century Cyprian wrote, "The day of pressure is even over our heads, and the consummation of all things and the coming of the Antichrist approaches."[18] A Jewish tradition from before the New Testament times, drawing a parallel from the six days of creation and the seventh day of rest, predicted that the world's history would continue six thousand years, followed by a Messianic era in the seventh millennium. Bishop Newton said "that the Jewish church before John, and the Christian Church after him, have believed and taught that these one thousand years will be the seventh Millenary of the world."[19] Already in A.D. 100 the Epistle of Barnabas

16 *Christian Missions and the Judgment of God* (SCM Press, 1953), p. 33, n. 12.

17 II Pet. 3:4.

18 Quoted by T. F. Glasson, *His Appearing and His Kingdom* (Epworth, 1953), p. 45.

19 Quoted by Peters, *op. cit.,* II, p. 448.

said that "in six thousand years shall all things be consummated."[20] Although the canonical books of the New Testament give no support for this date-setting device, it has been widely held through the centuries up to the present time. However, the chronology of the Septuagint, which was used in New Testament times and the centuries following, placed the beginning of human history in the year 5500 B.C. So the early chiliasts thought they were well through the sixth millennium. Those who have confidence today in this idea must accept the Usher chronology, which is probably not as nearly correct as was the Septuagint.

Augustine said, "It befits us not to know the remainder of the world's years. Some talk how it shall last 400, some 500, some 1,000 years after the Ascension." He recognized the folly of such speculation, for he said, "He scatters the fingers of all calculators, and bids them to be still."[21] But the calculation continued. Gregory the Great, who became pope in 590, thought the End was near because of "the most unspeakable Lombards."[22] Joachim of Flora, arguing from Revelation 11:3, thought the End would come in 1260. In 1530 Luther "was so convinced that the end was about to break with catastrophic swiftness that he resolved to publish his translation of Daniel right away in order that it might do its work before the mighty and terrible day of the Lord."[23] Later he figured that the Coming might be two or three hundred years away. The Anabaptist fanatic Melchior Hofman announced that the Lord would come to Strasbourg in 1533. Menno Simons set no dates.[24] "Servetus

20 *Ibid.*, p. 449.
21 Quoted by Glasson, *op. cit.*, p. 128, 19.
22 *Ibid.*, p. 45.
23 T. F. Torrance, "The Eschatology of the Reformation," in *Eschatology* (Oliver and Boyd, 1952), p. 43.
24 Roland H. Bainton, "The Enduring Witness," *Mennonite Life*, April, 1954.

computed the restitution would take place . . . in 1585."[25] "John Napier, the Scottish inventor of logarithms, predicted the Second Coming between the years 1668 and 1700."[26] John Wesley and the great commentator Bengel both set 1836 as the year for the Lord's return. William Miller, a founder of Seventh-Day Adventism, set 1843, and then 1844, as the day. Edward Irving said the Battle of Armageddon would be fought and Christ would come in 1868. The Dispensationalists widely accepted the seven-millenniums theory. "Six thousand year days of labor and then the Millennium, or blessed seventh thousand years of rest," wrote W. E. Blackstone.[27] One of the author's boyhood memories is a sermon in 1903 in which a visiting minister told the Kansas farmers it would be useless to sow wheat that fall, as the Lord would return before they could harvest it.

Very true still are the words of Sir Thomas Browne, of the seventeenth century, "That general opinion that the world grows near its end, hath possessed all ages as nearly as our own."[28]

Now all these prophets have proved to be mistaken. Surely we should have learned by now that date-setting is a foolish business. It is worse; it is wicked. For it adds to the Word of God. It puts the whole study of eschatology in disrepute, and deprives people of truth they ought to have as they turn from the calendar-makers in disgust.

I have come to the conclusion that one ought not say that Christ will come soon. If that saying would be inter-

25 Frank J. Wray, "The Anabaptist Doctrine of the Restitution of the Church," *Mennonite Quarterly Review*, July, 1954.

26 *Time*, April 19, 1954.

27 Quoted by W. H. Rutgers, *Premillennialism in America* (Goes, 1930), p. 163.

28 Quoted by Glasson, *op. cit.*, p. 44.

preted as meaning that He may come at any time, it would be true. But in our ordinary meaning of "soon," one just does not know that it is true. We know that He is coming, and we know that every day the Parousia is nearer. But we do not know that He is coming in our lifetime, nor in this decade or century. We must leave the time to God, who alone knows when the harvest is ripe. This is not mechanically or arbitrarily determined, but is dependent upon the relation of conditions in the world to the purpose of God. Obviously God would not be sovereign if we could tell Him the time when He must come. "His disciples," says R. B. Jones, "are to be passionate witnesses rather than program writers. They are to leave the times and seasons with Him while they prepare human hearts for the eventualities of the Day of the Lord."[29]

But are there not signs given by inspiration by which we may recognize the approach of the Day? Yes, there are. Jesus gave a number of signs, although in such a passage as Matthew 24 it is difficult to distinguish between the signs of the destruction of Jerusalem and the signs of the Parousia. We cannot list here all these signs. A good list is found in John C. Wenger's *Introduction to Theology*.[30] One of the clearest signs is that given by Jesus, that "this gospel of the kingdom shall be preached in the whole world for a testimony unto all the nations; and then shall the end come."[31] He did not say that all nations would accept the Gospel. Since we do not know exactly the degree of coverage this prediction requires, and since there has already been a world-wide preaching of the Gospel, we need not say that Christ could not come at any time. Evidently the early

29 *The Things Which Shall Be Hereafter* (Broadman, 1947), p. 162.
30 *Introduction to Theology* (Herald Press, 1954), pp. 335 f.
31 Matt. 24:14.

church, with its expectancy of the Parousia, did not feel that it had to wait on further evangelization. Much more widespread is the world evangel now, but the fact that He has not yet come must indicate that our task of evangelism is still incomplete.

Another prominent sign is the appearance of the Anti-christ. Since he is to be destroyed by the manifestation of Christ, evidently he must come on the scene before the Parousia. Since we do not know that he is here, we might argue that Christ cannot come just now. But when we remember that the Antichrist might be a system of thought or government, we cannot say for sure that he is not here.

Most of the signs given are of the things which have been here in some degree at various times throughout these "last days" since the First Advent. They may appear in greater magnitude and in greater concentration as the age draws to a close. For instance, the sign of war. W. M. Smith cites a study by Sorokin which shows "that the index of European wars grew from 2,678 in the twelfth century to 13,835.98 in the first twenty-five years of the twentieth century."[32]

It is easy to believe that we live in such a crisis of world turmoil as may indicate an early cataclysm. Jaspers says, "Intellectually, the consciousness of crisis reached its zenith with Kierkegaard and Nietzsche. Since their time the knowledge that we are at a turning point in history, at the termination of history in the existing sense, that we are witnessing the radical metamorphosis of humanity itself, has been gaining currency. After the First World War, it was no longer the sunset glow merely of Europe, but of all the cultures of the earth. An end of mankind, a recasting from which no people and no man was exempt—whether it

32 *World Crises and the Prophetic Scriptures* (Moody Press, 1952), p. 148.

was to annihilation, or to rebirth—could be felt. It was still not the end itself; but the knowledge of its possible imminence became prevalent."[33]

Thomas E. Murray, Atomic Energy Commissioner of the United States, after warning that man now holds within his hands the means to "completely exterminate the human race," says, "It may be the inscrutable will of God to make the twentieth century closing time for the human race."[34]

But while we must be aware that the End could come at any time, we must resist the temptation to take a look at the stresses and fears of our time, and then say, This is it. In 1914 C. I. Scofield wrote in the *Sunday School Times,* "If, then, Turkey and the Balkan states shall be drawn into the war now raging—then we may confidently answer that the war which is now drenching France, Poland, Belgium, and Germany with torrents of human blood, on a scale and with a remorselessness never before equaled in human history, does indeed mark the beginning of the end of this age."[35] The still bloodier World War II and forty years of history now make that prediction seem rather antiquated. We should be aware of any relevance of the signs to the times, but remember that the seasons are in the Father's hands. "It is Christ alone who will bring God's holy purpose to its glorious consummation, and it is God alone who knows when that will be. As Christians, therefore, we regard the signs of the times to be evidence of the fact that God works in an orderly way toward the goal of history, and we humbly trust in Christ, the Lord of history, to bring about that consummation."[36]

---

33 *The Origin and Goal of History* (Yale, 1953), p. 232.
34 *Time,* April 11, 1955.
35 Quoted by Alexander Reese, *op cit.,* p. 241.
36 Charles T. Fritsch, "The Message of Apocalyptic for Today," *Theology Today,* October, 1953.

The most emphatic word which Jesus speaks concerning the time is that it will be a surprise, that people will not be looking for it. It will be as in the days of Noah, when men were going about life in an unconcerned way, doing the usual things with never a thought of imminent disaster. Our danger, therefore, is that we will fall into this unconcern. And so we are told to watch, to be on the alert, to stay awake. The five foolish virgins were not watching portents in the skies; that was not their mistake. They were forgetful and unconcerned. Suddenness, unexpectedness—these are the characteristics of the Parousia. For everybody it will be like a thief coming in the night; somewhere on earth it will be every hour of the twenty-four.

We can only be certain that Christ is coming, and that He may come at any time. "It must be laid down as a first principle, that ever since the appearing of Christ, there is nothing left to the faithful, but with wakeful minds to be always intent on His Second Advent," said Calvin.[37] From the Ascension even until now, it has been the normal mood of the church to look for Him, to expect the Parousia. To imagine it very far away denies the lively sense of immediacy that is the essence of the blessed Hope.

The caretaker of a country estate kept the premises spick-and-span for the unpredictable visits of his master from the city. An observer said, "You act as if your master were coming tomorrow." "Today, sir, today!" was the answer of the faithful servant. "Watch therefore: for ye know not on what day your Lord cometh."[38] One cannot say a word on the subject to go beyond the simple wisdom of our Lord's warning. And the longer the waiting, the more the exhortation to watchfulness is needed.

37 Quoted by Peters, *ut supra*, III, p. 168.
38 Matt. 24:42.

G. Campbell Morgan had this sense of imminence when he said, "To me the Second Coming is the perpetual light on the path which makes the present bearable. I never lay my head on my pillow without thinking that, maybe, before morning breaks, the final morning may have dawned! I never begin my work without thinking that, perhaps, He may interrupt my work and begin His own. This is now His word to all believing souls, till He come. We are not looking for death; we are looking for Him!"[39] Those words do not sound foolish because Morgan has died. They would if he had said he would not die. They express exactly the attitude of a student of the Word and a believer in the eschatological promise. He never lost his consciousness that any day the promise might become reality. And he was always watching and ready.

39 Quoted in *Watchman-Examiner.*

XIII

THE MANNER
OF THE WAITING

As believing Christians we wait for our Lord. How shall
we wait? First, we wait in holy living. We are "like unto
men looking for their lord."[1] "Take care," Jesus said to His
disciples, "that your hearts are not loaded down with self-
indulgence and drunkenness and worldly cares, and that
day takes you by surprise, like a trap."[2] Paul links together
"looking for the blessed hope and appearing" and living
"soberly and righteously and godly in this present world."[3]
And Peter, after his picture of a fiery deluge and the coming
of a heaven and earth wherein righteousness dwells, concludes: "Wherefore, beloved, seeing that ye look for these
things, give diligence that ye may be found in peace, without spot and blameless in his sight."[4] And John says, after
telling us that when reality breaks through we shall see
Christ as He really is, "Everyone who has at heart a hope
like that keeps himself pure, for he knows how pure Christ
is."[5]

In the New Testament, we see how the expectation of the
Parousia is a powerful motive to good behavior. There
is holy fear and a consciousness of impending judgment.

1 Luke 12:36.
2 Luke 21:34 (Goodspeed).
3 Titus 2:12, 13.
4 II Pet. 3:13, 14.
5 I John 3:2, 3 (Phillips).

But there is more than that. There is a realization that the Christian is already living the life which is to come. Although he is in the old aeon, he is demonstrating the power of the new. The eschatological prospect makes conduct here at least semi-eschatological. It is the way of obedience and discipleship which leads to the rendezvous at the end. Martin Niemoeller puts it, "To follow Christ is to meet Him when He comes. If we do not follow Christ, we will miss Him when He comes."[6]

Here is the most powerful reasoning for being nonconformed to the world: we have been transferred from the kingdom of this age to the Kingdom of Him who has already redeemed us and who is coming again to make His reign absolute in the age to come. We are even now being oriented to eternal norms of conduct. We are learning the mores and the language of that City to which we are going. We are careful never to be involved in any manners that would mark us as belonging to the order which is passing away. A pilgrim people will have a pilgrim ethic. They derive their standards, not from the relative ethics of this world, but from the expressed will of their heavenly Lord. If those standards lead them into persecution or ridicule, they are not surprised. They live under the sign of the cross of Christ, and may through sufferings reach the place of eternal reward. For them, hope and obedience walk hand in hand. For them eschatology and ethics are inseparable. This world comes to know them as the people of another world, a people of God's own possession, who even in this world are ambitious only to please Him whom they shall serve eternally.

Our eternal vocation gives us a measuring stick for our vocations here. " 'In the last days' the truth about our jobs

6 Quoted in *The Mennonite*, Sept. 14, 1954.

and occupations will stand revealed for what it is eternally to God. Our human judgments on the worth or rewards of different kinds of daily work, on the marks of success in business and the professions—these judgments are not only individual; they are social and cultural as well. And 'at the end' when history becomes 'beyond history,' their distortions, snobbishness, and superficiality will be evident."[7]

The church on earth, we noticed earlier, has an interim function, between Pentecost and the Parousia. Likewise it has an interim ethic. But the interim is not, as Schweitzer thought, the short period between the First Coming and the time when Christ mistakenly supposed He would soon return. The interim is for the entire time between the two Comings, no matter how long that is. It is this, as Wendland says, "that gives Christian ethics its absolute character."[8] For the life lived now by God's people is derived from the life which they shall live eternally. So Christian ethics has an eternal quality. One cannot escape a New Testament command by relegating it to the brief period of the Primitive Church, or by postponing it to some future millennium when it becomes possible. Neither can one dismiss it as an impossible ideal, and be satisfied with choosing a lesser evil. That is a way of forgetting what age we really belong to. One who lives in the hope of the Parousia and the perfected Kingdom to come will not shrink, in spite of the difficulty, from submitting here and now to the heavenly rule. He will refuse, as J. H. Yoder says, "to eschatologize it out of the realm of his earthly living and doing."[9]

7 Cameron P. Hall, "Daily Work and Christian Vocation," *Christian Century,* July 28, 1954.

8 H. D. Wendland, quoted by W. Schweitzer, *Eschatology and Ethics* (World Council of Churches, Geneva, 1951), p. 8.

9 "The Anabaptist Dissent," *Concern,* June, 1954, p. 61.

Otherwise the world can well doubt that we have any hope beyond history. Those who succeed in adjusting themselves very comfortably to this age can hardly have a prophetic message about another age. "When those who know Him," says Paul Peachey, "no longer reveal an awareness that 'it is a terrible thing to fall into the hands of the living God,' those who don't know Him need not worry about getting acquainted with Him."[10] A terrible contradiction would be a theoretical interest in eschatology that produces no effect upon the ethical character. How can we hear from one mouth, "Maranatha," and "Nay, Lord." The doctrine of eschatology and the ethics of the new aeon belong together. "I Corinthians 13 is inconceivable in the present except in the future context of I Corinthians 15, and I Corinthians 15 is just a display of intellectual fireworks about the future without its present basis in I Corinthians 13."[11]

One can easily see why the questions of time and manner of the Coming, which have largely occupied many, are of little importance. "The question is not, When will our Lord return? but How shall I behave until He does return? Conduct and not time is the pivot upon which all Christ's exhortations turned."[12] If the servant knew the time of the master's return, said Jesus, he would not watch and would fall into evil ways. Calvin said that "in the service of God, which in the corruption of our nature is a more than difficult matter, we are kept and established by the expectation of Christ; otherwise the world drags us back to itseslf, and we grow weary."[13]

10 "Toward an Understanding of the Decline of the West," *Concern, ut supra,* p. 40.
11 J. E. Fison, *The Christian Hope* (Longmans, 1954), p. 126.
12 Geo. P. Eckman, *When Christ Comes Again* (Abingdon, 1917), p. 146.
13 Quoted by Geo. H. N. Peters, *Theocratic Kingdom* (Kregel, 1952), III, p. 322.

Since deceit is to be so widely used in the days of Antichrist, since many shall fall away from the faith, it is especially important that as the hour grows later believers should in real concentration set their minds upon the truth and their hearts upon the will of God. It is possible for one to fall into apostasy of thought and life almost without being aware of it. It is a time to test ourselves and others by the pure Word of God.

We wait for the Parousia, then, in holy living, and, second, in active service. It has been often charged, especially in America, that occupation with eschatology unfits one for responsibility in the service of God, even for everyday duties. A current popular song expresses a carelessness about keeping the house in repair in view of the meeting of the saints in the air. There were some at Thessalonica who were sitting around waiting for the Parousia. Paul, who was also looking for Christ, told them to go to work. There is a danger of a certain kind of apocalypticism making people irresponsible. But true eschatology is always a call to action, never to retreat. "Neither with Paul nor with the other apostles," says Kantonen, "does the hope of the imminent coming of the Lord lead to a fanatical preoccupation with the future at the expense of what needs to be done in the present."[14] Instead of blunting the social sense, says Paul Minear, "current efforts to understand New Testament eschatology result in an ethic that is too radical for the contemporary church, in an appraisal of social duties that is altogether too realistic and too sobering."[15]

We need in this time, not less eschatology in our religious diet, but more, in order that our service to God may have the stimulus of the Christian hope. Paul S. Rees, a former

14 T. A. Kantonen, *The Christian Hope* (Muhlenberg, 1954), p. 18.
15 "In Whom Do We Hope?" *Christian Century*, Jan. 27, 1954.

president of the National Association of Evangelicals, after admitting that a small minority of evangelicals have yielded to "an enervating lassitude, an unproductive, benumbing pessimism, an otherworldly quietism," insists that "the authentic breed of evangelical believes in the paradox of the present and absent Christ. . . . He believes that until the Great Day dawns he should work with passionate devotion to bring all men to put their trust in God through Christ, to receive Him as their Saviour, to serve Him in the fellowship of His church, and to make known His justice, goodness, and truth in the vocations of the common life."[16]

The parable of the talents shows clearly that during the interim of the Lord's absence a task has been set for His servants. And it will go ill with that servant who in carelessness, or pessimism, or laziness, or lack of love buries his talent in the earth and thus awaits his Lord's coming. The conclusion to the great resurrection chapter in I Corinthians is a call to ethical strength and vigorous work: "Continue to be firm, incapable of being moved, always letting the cup run over in the work of the Lord, because you know that your labor in the service of the Lord is never thrown away."[17] No note there of ascetic withdrawal, of giving up in defeat, of social irresponsibility! "History, from Abraham to Marx, demonstrates that significant action, for good or for evil, is accomplished by those whose present action is illuminated by an eschatological hope. . . . Schweitzer's thesis, generally accepted by liberal theologians, that the eschatological expectancy of the early church led to ethical irresponsibility, is simply wrong, exegetically and historically."[18]

16 "Exploiting Our Opportunity," *United Evangelical Action*, 1954.
17 I Cor. 15:58 (Williams).
18 J. H. Yoder, "Peace Without Eschatology?" Unpublished paper, p. 8.

For what do we labor? To bring to bear the claims and demands of Christ with reference to every human situation. We seek to make heard throughout the world Christ's condemnation of sin and His offer of salvation to all sinners. We do not hesitate to apply the searching ethic of Christ to the evils of our day, no matter how long they may have been covered over by nominal Christian approval. War, economic oppression, racial and class discrimination, self-seeking pleasure—these are wrong because Christ condemns them, and we strive to make His condemnation heard. The World Missionary Conference at Tambaram said, "The church of Christ . . . cannot pass by the sufferings of the world; it is bound to comfort and heal the sick and downtrodden, to help and strengthen the poor and heavy-laden, to fight against injustice and social evils, to awaken the conscience of nations and mankind and so to be the light and salt of the world."[19] We do what we find needs to be done, taking seriously every problem and task. Against insuperable difficulties we work, careless of what happens to us, only knowing that the Gospel must be made known and every suffering one must receive the cup of water in the name of Christ.

We do not do this to preserve the present order of society from dissolution, or even to "build the Kingdom of God." We have no imperative to do either. We are keenly aware that our Lord's Kingdom, although it has a constant relevance to this world, does not belong to it. We have no enthusiasm for a "social gospel" which is enamored of "a paradise of chromium fittings, super-cinemas, and refrigerators," as Alan Richardson described "the kingdom of

---

19 Quoted by W. Schweitzer, *Eschatology and Ethics* (World Council of Churches, Geneva, 1951), p. 16.

man."[20] But as ambassadors of the Kingdom of God we proclaim the message of that Kingdom. We have no illusions that it will be universally accepted. We expect to find the perfected Kingdom only after the Parousia. But we do see many accepting the Lord and learning His ways. We see the darkness broken here and there by the light of the New Age. We see some evils being eliminated, such as slavery and racism. At this we rejoice, for we know they are contrary to God's righteousness. We are glad for every triumph of Christ whether here or beyond the Parousia.

Our chief task is evangelization. Even though we see wickedness increase, it is our passion to preach the Gospel to all. This above everything else was the responsibility laid upon His disciples by our Lord when He went away. The Great Commission sets the program for this age. As long as there are people who have not opened their hearts to the Gospel, we know what to do. This is our uncompleted assignment. "Our discussions on the nature of the church and the content of the Christian hope will be barren if they do not result in an inescapable summons to proclamation and a new obedience which will thrust the church forth into the world as an expectant and evangelizing community in this generation."[21] Eschatology gives to evangelism a sense of urgency which can come from no other inspiration. And because Christ will come to the whole world, the fruit of the Gospel must be gathered from amongst all nations. The Pentecost miracle broke down every barrier of language, and the missionary proclamation in this age knows no favorite people or chosen race. Because the task is long and difficult, we may get weary and long for the land of rest. But "we have no right to our Sabbath ease and our prom-

20 Quoted by Warren C. Young, "The Christian Hope and the Social Order," *Mennonite Quarterly Review*, April, 1954.
21 C. W. Ranson, quoted in *The Mennonite*, Sept. 14, 1954.

ised end before the Gospel will have been preached throughout the world."22 The prospect of the coming of the Lord
to begin His judgment at the household of God may well
strike fear into the hearts of wealthy congregations worshiping in temples and giving only dimes and quarters to
world evangelization.

In a certain Greek church one sees, on leaving the building, a picture of the Second Coming. It is a reminder to
the worshipers to return to the daily tasks with eternity always in view.

In the third place, we wait for the Parousia in loving anticipation. By Christian faith we are brought into relation
to a Person. The Person is Christ, who is not only an object
toward which understanding is directed, but a living reality
of one to whom we are bound by the closest ties of affection.
"Lovest thou me?" was His question to Peter, as if that were
more important than "What do you think about me?" To
be sure, involved in Peter's love was his conviction that Jesus was the Christ, the Son of the Living God. But the
creedal commitment was not enough. Peter had to come
also to the place of personal affection. His confidence grew
into love.

The Apostle John, whom Jesus loved, says much more
about love than do the other evangelists. And he is also the
one who says more about the realized, as compared to the
future, aspects of Christ's work for us. His fuller presenta-
tion of the inner, spiritual phases of Christ's ministry has
a direct relation to the love between Christ and those who
believe in Him. The much wider perspective which the
later Gospel can have gives an emotional depth to it. So it
is in the context of love that John speaks of the Parousia.

Paul speaks of those who love the Appearing, the Par-

22 T. O. Wedel, *Evangelism,* a mimeographed address released at Evanston.

ousia. There is a striking contrast between this love and that of the next verse, the love of Demas for this present age.[23] What a waste of affection, to pour it out upon an age which is passing away! And what a rich use for affection, to fix it upon a meeting with a Loved One with whom we are permitted to spend an eternity! Paul's figure of the bride and bridegroom, a figure which Jesus also used, accentuates the warmly personal quality of the waiting for the Day of meeting. This is a Day to be desired, not dreaded. It is the wedding day, not the doomsday. Fison develops this theme in great detail in his book, *The Christian Hope*. Here is a typical passage: "Just as a lover will prepare for a date and a rendezvous with his beloved, so we (if we in any way love our Lord Jesus Christ) will prepare for that day of meeting, not as if it would be like the medieval *Dies irae, dies illa,* but as if it would be (as indeed it will be) a meeting with one who knows the secrets of all hearts . . . by the natural sympathy of a true lover."[24]

The natural prayer of one who looks forward to a lovers' meeting is, "Come quickly, Lord Jesus, come." And such a one is not going to fill the waiting hours with blueprints and time schedules. He will be so occupied in mind with the Person to be met that he will have no thought for such extraneous matters. The What? and the How? yield to the Whom? "The study of prophecy is valueless, it is of the flesh, it is but wood, hay, and stubble unless it is motivated by the holy desire for consummation,"[25] by a lively expectation of the Beloved One. Meeting Him, as Neander said, is "fitted to be, not an object of dread, but of joyful, longing hope."[26]

23 II Tim. 4:8, 9.
24 *Op. cit.,* p. 49.
25 E. E. English, *Re-Thinking the Rapture* (Southern Bible Book House, Travelers Rest, S. C., 1954), p. 27.
26 Quoted by Geo. H. N. Peters, *op. cit.,* I, p. 477.

And that word brings us to the fourth way in which we wait for Him: in certain hope. The concept of hope is central and all-pervasive in the New Testament. In the Acts and Epistles alone the noun "hope" is used forty-eight times. Our present English usage gives little hint of its true meaning. Hope for us means little more than a desire. A girl may have a hope chest who has no certainty whatever that she will ever use its contents in a home of her own. But in the New Testament hope is "a dead certainty." "Christian hope," says Newbigin, "is an utterly unshakable assurance of that which shall be because God has promised it, which is sure even though our desire for it should faint and grow weary."[27]

Human hope is self-engendered. Shelley describes the method:

"to hope till Hope creates
From its own wreck the thing it contemplates."[28]

But hope created thus can by the same method be destroyed. Only in Christian faith does hope rest on a foundation strong enough to support it under stress and pressure. For Christian hope rests on God, whose goodness, mercy, and power have been amply demonstrated, and can be relied upon. "Hope in God does not refer to a vague future possibility. Because God's purpose is everlasting, hope springs from the reality of what He has done and is doing, and not simply from the notion that He might do something else. What he will do is fully consistent with what He has been doing all the while. . . . What is about to happen among men is the accomplishment of a 'word' that He has already

---

27 Quoted by Paul S. Minear, *Christian Hope and the Second Coming* (Westminster, 1954), p. 26.

28 *Adonais.*

spoken, a program of action that He has already set under way."[29]

Hope is a sure and steadfast anchor to the soul, then, because it rests on God. In the Maya language, E. A. Nida tells us, to hope in God is to "hang onto God."[30] Only as God has planted His hope in our hearts can we have hope. It is the historic assurance of the incarnational ministry of Christ and the experiential assurance which comes from being crucified and risen with Him that brings us to know the hope. The God who can and has done what we already have experienced can and will do all He has promised.

Not all hope, of course, refers to matters eschatological. God's complete redemptive purpose is the hope set before us. It involves all that being saved involves: atonement, justification, sanctification, Spirit-indwelling, ultimate transformation. But in many places it does clearly and specifically refer to the *eschaton,* by which the redemptive program of God shall be completely realized.

How can we be sure of something that has not yet happened? On the basis of what has already happened. The *eschaton* has already begun. The First Advent is the beginning of a series of events that shall go on to a Second Advent. He who once came will, according to the same purpose and power which brought Him then, come again. His resurrection was a first stage which must go on to the resurrection of all. The Kingdom inaugurated must be fully manifested. The earnest of the Spirit must be made good by a full-blown spiritual experience. We are not waiting for something that may happen. We are waiting for the completion of something surely and gloriously begun. So surely and so gloriously will it end.

29 Paul S. Minear, *op. cit.,* p. 26.
30 E. A. Nida, *God's Word in Man's Language* (Harper, 1952), p. 133.

Karl Heim has used the figure of the lightning and the thunder. Both come from the same discharge of electricity. There is an interval between them so far as our perception is concerned. But when once the lightning has flashed, surely the thunder will roll. There is only the little period of tense waiting. So, once God has invaded our world in the Incarnation, the Resurrection, and the outpouring of the Spirit, the complementary invasion of the Parousia will surely come. The light of the first is the cause of the power of the second.[31]

What the Parousia will mean for us we have already seen. There is good reason why that should be our happiest Day —completed redemption for us and to our God the glory which is His due. In that hope we need have no worries or fears about ourselves, and no doubts about God's ultimate triumph. With such ultimate hope, we can more easily live without the immediate hopes of which our times deprive us.

Christian hope shows most brightly against the backdrop of darkness in which we live today. Bertrand Russell has expressed our dominant pessimism: "Over man and all his works night falls pitiless and dark." There are fears and frustrations on every hand, and the pall of atomic destruction hangs over us. Woodrow Wilson's book on the League of Nations was called *The Hope of the World*. Many other hopes have been blown to pieces since his. A world which has no hope tries dope. Many take refuge in nihilism, which admits the entire meaninglessness of life. Some are led by their philosophy to suicide. Others attempt a heroic existence that has no consolation, no assurance, no hope.

God has something better for us. It is the age-old hope set forth in the Scriptures. A Fife laborer said to Robert Louis Stevenson, "Him that has aye something ayont, need

31 T. A. Kantonen, *op. cit.*, p. 78.

never be weary."[32] The Christian has something beyond. He has Someone there, Someone he knows. He has a Lord and Saviour in heaven, who has given him life and hope through His life, death, and resurrection. This Saviour has promised to come to receive us unto Himself, that where He is we may be also. On this earth we do not know what is coming, but we know Who is coming.[33] In history we may be on the losing side. But beyond history we shall be on the winning side. We live now only in the "land of promise." We look for "the city which hath the foundations, whose builder and maker is God."[34] Not even concentration camps and communist prisons and shadows of atomic clouds can take away the confidence of one who can muse upon the hope of an *eschaton* that our Omega is bringing.

The drama of the ages, God's redemptive action, will end in such eternal blessedness as an Old English bard expressed:

"Let us muse in our hearts on the heavenly mansions,
 Thitherward planning our pilgrimage,
 Seeking the way to the blessed stronghold
 Of life and joy in the love of the Lord.
 And thanks be to God, the Giver of glory,
 The Lord Everlasting, the Holy King,
 Who hath granted us honor through ages to come."[35]

32 Quoted by Archibald M. Hunter, "The Hope of Glory," *Interpretation*, April, 1954.

33 Evanston "Message," *Christian Century*, Sept. 22, 1954.

34 Heb. 11:10.

35 *The Seafarer.*